WAMPUM

by

ANNE MOLLOY

*Illustrated with prints
and photographs*

HASTINGS HOUSE, PUBLISHERS

NEW YORK

PICTURE ACKNOWLEDGMENTS Albany Institute of History and Art, 85; Detroit, Michigan, Public Library, Burton Historical Collection, 30; John B. Knox, Knox Family, Inc., 60; Library of Congress, 28, 52; Nina Fletcher Little, Brookline, Mass., 78; McCord Museum, 19, 56 (2nd); Museum of the American Indian, Heye Foundation, 44, 50, 56 (1st), 72, 76, 90, 100, 110, 111; Museum of Art, Rhode Island School of Design, Providence, R.I. (Gift of Mr. Robert Winthorp), 34; The National Gallery of Canada, Ottawa, 98; National Museums of Canada, 52, 56 (4th), 80, 81, 83; The New York Public Library, 8, 10, 12, 16, 18, 21, 29, 40 (bottom), 95; NYPL Rare Books Division, 24, 42, 65; NYPL Stokes Collection, 15; New York State Museum, Albany, 40 (top), 71; Pennsylvania Academy of the Fine Arts, 89; *Pontiac, King of the Great Lakes,* 22; Royal Ontario Museum, 70; The Smithsonian Institution, 56 (3rd), 108; The Smithsonian Institution National Anthropological Archives, 69, 106; Tarrantine Club, Bangor, Maine, 117

LIBRARY OF CONGRESS CATALOGING IN PUBLICATION DATA
Molloy, Anne Stearns Baker, 1907–   Wampum.
    Bibliography: p.   Includes index.
    SUMMARY: Describes the history of wampum and how it gained importance as currency
and as a sacred record of tribal history.
    1. Wampum—Juvenile literature. 2. Indians of North America—Money—Juvenile literature. [1. Wampum. 2. Indians of North America—Money] I. Title.
E98.M7M64   970'.004'97   76-26870
ISBN 0-8038-8079-0 lib. bdg.

Published simultaneously in Canada by
Saunders of Toronto, Ltd., Don Mills, Ontario
Printed in the United States of America

Contents

Acknowledgments

For the making of this book many persons patiently answered questions and provided, either from the institutions with which they are associated or from their own resources, both information and photographic material. Among those who must be thanked for their courtesy and kindness are the following: Mrs. Frances Wagner, Albany Institute of Art; Mrs. Bernice S. Sprenger and Mrs. Alice C. Dalligan, Burton Historical Collection, Detroit Public Library; Ms. Phyllis Rabineau, Dept. of Anthropology, Field Museum; James V. Ciaramitaro, Curator, Ft. Wayne Military Museum; Carmelo Guadagno, S. Alexandride, Photographic Dept., Museum of the American Indian; Conrad E. W. Graham, Registrar, McCord Museum; Mrs. Marjorie E. Colt, Museum of Art, Rhode Island School of Design; Ms. Kathleen Bishop-Glover and Denis B. Alsford, Acting Curator and Curator of Collections, National Museums of Canada; Philip C. Gifford, Museum of Natural History; Mrs. Valerie Simpson, New Brunswick Museum; Ms. Margaret Caesar, New Jersey State Museum; John G. Broughton, Assistant Commissioner for Cultural Education, Charles E. Gillette, Curator of Anthropology, and Donna Momrow, New York State Museum and Science Service; Ms. Sally Bond, Ms. Denise Batts, Peabody Museum of Archaeology and Ethnology, Harvard University; Ms. Yoshiko Yamamoto, Peabody Museum of Natural History, Yale University; Ms. Kathy Zickler, Pennsylvania Academy of Fine Arts; Mrs. Ursula Young, Ms. Avril Dempster, Ethnology Dept., Royal Ontario Museum; Mrs. Barbara Stuckenrath, Dept. of Anthropology, Smithsonian Institution; Albina De Meio, Keeper of Collections, American Section, The University Museum, University of Pennsylvania; The Tarratine Club, Bangor Maine; John B. Knox, President, Knox Family, Inc.; Mrs. Nina Fletcher Little.

Wampum Belts

IN AMERICAN AND CANADIAN MUSEUMS

The museums, historical societies, and the libraries listed below all have wampum pieces in their American Indian collections. Many own splendid belts of which the more famous and fascinating are named.

District of Columbia
The Smithsonian Institution
The Great Wampum Belt of Union, symbolizing the consolidation of midwestern tribes under Tecumseh after 1800.

New Jersey
New Jersey State Museum Cultural Center, Trenton
A purple wampum belt edged with red glass beads.

Ohio
The Ohio State Historical Society Center, Columbus
Wyandot peace belt.

Michigan
Detroit Public Library, Detroit
Belt accompanying the 1769 deed to Belle Isle.
Detroit Historical Museum, Detroit
Wampum belt recording the transfer of land to Major Robert Rogers in 1760.

Massachusetts
Peabody Museum of Archaeology and Ethnology, Cambridge

Pennsylvania
The University Museum, University of Pennsylvania, Philadelphia

New York
The American Museum of Natural History, New York City
Mohican belt used in trading with early Dutch settlers. A purple wampum belt with eight figures—a man, a woman, two crosses, four wigwams—used by the Penobscot as a marriage proposal belt.
Heye Foundation, Museum of the American Indian, New York City

Penn Treaty belts given to William Penn at the Treaty of Shackamaxon, 1683.

Condolence belt of the Wolf Clan of the Seneca, probably
18th century.

Five Nations war belt used before the Tuscarora joined the
League.

Oldest belt known to which a definite date can be given
(Huron).

Belt fragment reputedly part of the *Great White Belt of De-
kanawida* used during the formation of the Iroquois League.

Condolence belt marking the death of Caty Hoffmann, 1775
and given to her father by the Six Nations.

Belt of Joseph Brant commemorating his journey to England
in 1775.

Belt of Black Hawk, leader in the Black Hawk War of 1832.

New York State Museum, Albany

The most famous of its twenty six splendid belts are:

The Hiawatha Belt	First Palefaces Belt
The Washington Covenant Belt	Stanwix Treaty Belt

Illinois

The Field Museum of Natural History, Chicago

Oneida belt from Chief Skenandoa's ancient buckskin bag.

A Black Hawk belt.

Two Penobscot "marriage belts."

Belt of Molly Molasses, Penobscot medicine woman.

Canada

The McCord Museum, Montreal

A belt commemorating the conversion of a tribe to Christianity.
A Huron belt commemorating the mission church of Ossosne,
1638.

The Museum of Man, the National Museums of Canada, Ottawa

Iroquois treaty belt made after the end of the war. One of the
two figures is "laying down the hatchet."

The Royal Ontario Museum, Toronto

A Six Nations Iroquois belt of purple beads with two figures
depicting bowls for beavertail soup.

Iroquois belt buried with others for safekeeping during the
Colonial War between 1680 and 1700.

6

Foreword

When the old sea captain's desk first came into our household, the small drawers at the top were stuffed with pencils and compasses, erasers, steel pen points and, more unusual, a small book of gold leaf sheets and a short string of flat, white beads cut from sea shells.

"The family wampum," my mother called these beads as airily as if every household had some. As a matter of fact, she knew no more than we did about them. We imagined that they came from the New Hampshire farming side of the family and not the sea-faring one. Perhaps, we thought, they came from the great-grandmother who had been somewhat of an herb doctor and healer. Some of her herbal medicines came from the Indians, so perhaps the beads did, too.

Then one day several years ago, I saw a belt of similar beads lying in a museum case. My heart jumped. Not that the belt was beautiful in itself—far from it. Its ends petered out untidily in bare leather strings. It was a long woven strip of white beads like the one we had. But in it were woven dark figures of men holding hands as do paper dolls cut from one piece of paper. The last manikin at one end was cut down the center. The belt hinted powerfully and mysteriously of meanings that could only be imagined. I wanted to know what they were.

From that time on, I have kept an eye open for the word "wampum" in my reading, an ear alert for any mention of it in the conversation of those who collect Indian artifacts.

That is how the book began.

I have been constantly surprised as I gathered information about wampum at how often those who witnessed its use told of it in their accounts. And that use was more widespread than I had dreamed. It touched the lives of European kings, powerful sachems, hopeful bridegrooms in the tribes of northeast Maine and thirsty troopers of the Army of the West, pressing on to take over California from Spain. It played a part in the lives of ordinary folk like my New Hampshire grandparents, as well.

What follows are the highlights of its story.

The manner of their fishing.

A Cannow.

CHAPTER ONE

From Shells to Beads

❦

INDIAN TRIBES living near the north Atlantic coast left their inland villages and their cornfields and flocked to the shore for the warm summer months.

During the long days of sunshine or soft fog, they feasted on food from the sea. They ate clams and mussels and other shellfish. They caught fish with wicker traps and nets made from vegetable fibers. In shallow waters near shore, they speared large lobsters and caught crabs. Some of the more hardy launched seagoing canoes to spear porpoises and even whales. When the sojourn by the shore was done, the women packed up dried and smoked fish in birchbark or woven ash baskets. Then they turned their backs on the sea until the next year.

As a reminder of their visits, the Indians left behind great mounds of shells from the crustaceans they had eaten. These were not formed in one season. Tribes returned summer after summer and over the decades, the piles grew ever higher. Many remain in place today.

But not every shell was left for waste. Some were carried away to use in winter villages. Indians discovered very early that shells could, without too much toil, become tools and utensils.

9

Fishing methods used by the Roanoke Indians of Virginia in 1500's.

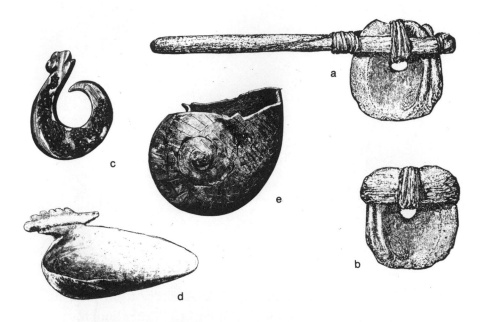

Sea shells made these tools and utensils: (a) *a war club,* (b) *a scraper,* (c) *a fish hook,* (d) *a spoon,* (e) *a cup.*

Stout surf clam shells were fashioned into cups, spoons and sippers. A strong shell bound with sinews to a stick made a more efficient hoe than the stick alone.

Some shells became sharp with only a bit of grinding—sharp enough to skin game or scrape clean the hides of beaver, deer, and bear, and smaller creatures as well. And sharp enough to use in grooming. Women hacked their hair short with mussel shells and men used pieces of shells as razors or tweezers to rid their faces of hair.

Tribes living beside New England's warmer waters, on the underside of Cape Cod and along Long Island Sound, discovered that a conch shell made a fine trumpet. Some coast-dweller must have picked up one with a broken spire from the sand and blown into the hole. He heard a sound that was strong and, with the power of his lungs behind it, could be heard a long distance. Conch shells became widely used for sending messages of greeting or warning. Later, the conch trumpet joined the skin-headed drum, the gourd and the tortoise shell rattle in making solemn music for tribal dances.

Tribes treasured shells for their beauty as much as for their usefulness. Shells had pearly, shimmering tints, and they were not fleeting or fragile like flowers, butterflies or the bright plumage of birds.

No one knows when Indians first thrust splinters of shell through their noses or lips, or when they started to sew decorative shells to their garments. Nor do we know when they began to make beads out of shells. The first Europeans who came along the north Atlantic coast early in the 17th century found Indians wearing strings of shell beads around their necks and wrists and dangling from their earlobes. To the visiting white men, they were merely "curious works." The explorers could not foresee that they themselves would become involved with shell beads.

The makers of shell beads along the northeastern shores were all Algonkian-speaking people. Roughly, they can be divided into three groups. One was made up of tribes in southern Connecticut and Rhode Island, principally the Pequot and the Narragansett. Another group lived clustered near the southern coast of New York and northeast New Jersey. They were the Unami Lenape, later called the Delaware. A third group of bead makers lived on Long Island, which they called "the land of loose shells." The Montauk were the most powerful, and probably the most flourishing of the Montauk group were the Matinecock. Along with the Rockaway, the Massapequa, the Setauket and the Manhasset, they left their names on the island.

Nearly all the shores of the northeast were rich in shells. But only certain shells were made into beads—those soft enough to work and not so brittle they splintered into tiny bits. For the most part, the Indians used whelk shells which lay for the taking in windrows on the shore. From seaweed coils along the high tide mark, they shook loose the Channelled Whelk, with its

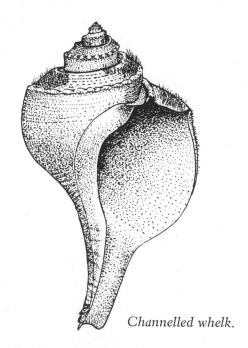

Channelled whelk.

flat, twisting whorls, the smaller Waved Whelk with its interior enamelled a soft yellow, and the Knobby Whelk. The last had an orange-red lining and, because it was larger than the others and provided more beads, was most often used. They also bartered for the Paper Fig Whelk, named for its thin shell, which came from warmer waters to the south.

Finding shells was easy. Turning them into beads took a great deal of time and patience. The task, especially the drilling, probably fell to the women. A worker knocked out the pieces of shell she wanted with a stone, laid one upon flat rock and ground it with sand until it was roughly round in shape. Then, she did the tedious drilling of a hole through the circular piece, first at one end, then the other until the two holes met, always at a slight angle. She probably used a very simple tool—a pointed sliver of slate, perhaps, or a sharpened stick. Then, she might grind the bead again on sand-covered stone to smooth its surface.

These early beads, which archaeologists called *disc* beads, resembled in shape a leather washer of the sort used in present day faucets. They varied in size, from $\frac{1}{10}$ of an inch to two inches in diameter, and from $\frac{1}{30}$ of an inch to two inches in thickness.

A worker strung her beads into necklaces, bracelets or eardrops. For larger beads, she used animal sinews or shredded deerskin as thread. When bead holes were small, she used plant fibres—dogbane stems or those of milkweed and often the shredded bark of the slippery elm tree. These fibres made line strong enough for fishing and had strength enough for even the largest beads.

The women of the bead-making tribes took pleasure in adorning themselves and their families. They could have no foreboding of what an important part these simple objects they made would play in the future of their people.

Three stages in turning a shell's column into beads.

CHAPTER TWO

Henry Hudson and the Dutch

❧ ❦

THE INDIANS who saw it were startled by Henry Hudson's ship, the *Half Moon*, as it sailed into New York Bay in 1609. Some thought it was a winged creature from the skies. To others, it was a monster from the deep. But many overcame their awe and set out in their canoes for a cautious visit.

The crew hung over the bulwarks to watch them come. The mate, Robert Juet, later wrote his impressions: "The people of the countrey came aboard of us, . . . and brought greene tobacco, and gave us of it for knives and beads." The canoes also carried corn, freshly harvested. And they offered the newcomers hemp twisted into rope.

The crew noticed the shell ornaments of their visitors, but what really held the attention of the Dutchmen were the furs the Indians wore. One man, a good judge of furs, blew into the hairs of several beaver robes to part them. The down was thick and lustrous. This was the best beaver. Others of the crew examined the deer, raccoon and wild cat garments their visitors wore.

As for the captain, Hudson could not forget those splendid furs. They lingered in his mind even longer than the teeming

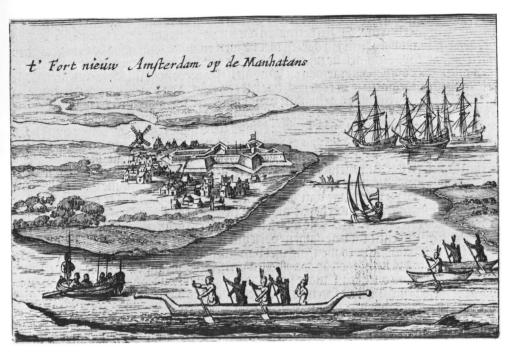

New Amsterdam, now New York, as it looked in the early days of Dutch settlement.

shoals of fish which had so impressed him as he ranged the coast of Newfoundland. He was not content until the Dutch sent him once again to New York Bay.

He returned to Holland with a cargo so rich that his Dutch employers decided to maintain a fur trading post on Manhattan Island. For the most part, the people they sent as colonists were Walloons. Their history was similar to that of the Pilgrims. They, too, had suffered religious persecution and had left their homes in Flanders to settle in the Dutch city of Leiden. They too, had not prospered. When the offer came from Dutch officials to send them as colonists to the New World, they seized it.

Although the Walloons themselves did not grow rich, their Dutch sponsors did. In one cargo alone they received 7,256 beaver skins from the New World. Encouraged by rich rewards, a group of Dutchmen bought Manhattan Island from the Algonkian tribe, the Canarsee. There, they carried on a vigorous fur trade with the Indians.

15

What a pity that the Indians who first stared at newcomers to their land did not write down how the strangers looked to them. What did they think of those starched ruffs and tabs, the confining armor, and above all, those monstrous steeple hats? In the few portraits painted of Indians in the days of colonial settlement, not one of the subjects wears a hat. He may wear an article or two of white man's clothing—a coat or even breeches —but for some reason, never a hat.

Walloon settlers building on the Hudson River at Ft. Orange where Albany now stands.

These seventeenth century Europeans are wearing fashionable hats of felted beaver fur.

Although the Indians did not know it in the beginning, there was a strong link between the white man's hat and their own shell beads. In Europe, hats made from glossy felted beaver fur were the rage. And, because only the wealthy could afford them, they became a symbol of success. As a result, European beaver, except for diminishing stocks in Russia and Sweden, were soon trapped out. This is why the sight of fine beaver pelts had so excited the men of the *Half Moon* as their Indian visitors came aboard. The sailors knew that in Europe, men were as greedy for beaver pelts as they were for gold.

Even when an influx of thousands of beaver pelts a year came from the New World, the price of beaver hats stayed high. Fathers willed their hats to their sons. An Englishman called "Beau" Nash set the fashion by owning a beaver hat so large that he never dared take it off in public for fear of it being stolen.

Remarkably, the shell beads so casually noted by Henry Hudson's men helped tremendously in furthering trade. The Dutch

Barter between Indians and settlers.

traders soon learned what commodities—metal tools, guns, powder, liquor, blankets—the Indians liked in exchange for their
furs. Soon they realized, although they never fully understood
why, that shell beads had as much appeal as any commodity
they could provide.

When they saw Indians using the beads for barter they be-
lieved them to be using money. They quickly adopted the de-
vice and put a precise, fixed value upon a certain measure of
beads. Indians accepted this value, and trade increased between
the two groups. In fact, there soon was a greater demand for
beads than there was a supply of them.

In the beginning, the Dutch called the shell beads *sewant*.
This is what they understood the bead makers along the coasts

to be calling them. The Montauk name for Long Island was *sewounhocky*. For some reason the Dutch who heard it thought they were speaking of shell beads and adopted this Indian word for them, shortening it to *sewant*.

As for the Indians, their own name for the beads was *wampumpoeag,* sometimes heard as *wampumpeag*. It is a chain of three words. The first part, *wamp* means white. The second, *umpe* or *ope* means anything strung on a cord. And lastly there is *ag* or *ak* which, when added to a word, makes it plural. In time, men from Europe adopted a shortened version of the long Algonkian word. They clipped it to *wampum*.

When they first came to the New World, the tidy Dutch, accustomed to the finest manufactured goods, found the Indian beads crude. And, once the Dutch saw that shell beads would help them acquire furs, they realized that bead-making was tediously slow. As soon as they could, they provided Indian workers with metal awls or drills made in Holland.

Early flat disc beads, longer cylindrical beads and glass ones strung together.

Mounted in wooden shafts, the new drills pierced beads much faster than the primitive ones and they made much more attractive beads. It was now possible to make longer, cylindrical beads. They were generally twice as long as they were wide and they are known today as cylindrical or *council* wampum. European string soon replaced vegetable sinews and fibre, in these new style wampums.

Indians called their metal drills "muxes," (or "muges" or mucx," depending on the ear of the white man recording the word.) We don't know the Algonkian name for the stones upon which they ground and polished shell pieces. Apparently, they were not a commonly found variety of stone. Traders carried them as stock in trade to supply bead makers.

When William Bartlett, a fur buyer of New London, died in 1658, he left 9 "Indian matts," a quantity of wampum and 3 "wampum stones" among other goods. Each stone was valued at one shilling twopence. One Long Island deed states that Montauk leaders demand 100 "muxes" for the land where East Hampton now stands. And, in western New Jersey, when a group of Delaware parted with land lying between Oldman's and Timber Creeks in 1677, they asked for 120 awl blades.

In the days of disc bead making, when drills were primitive— pointed sticks or slivers of stone—methods were simple. A worker squatted on his haunches, held an undrilled bead in one hand and, with the other hand, rolled the shaft of the mounted stone or the stick along his thigh. Or he set his drill point in the center of a bead piece as it lay upon a flat stone and rotated the shaft briskly between his palms. This is known as "palm drilling."

Later, with metal awls, more elaborate drilling methods came into use. One was "bow drilling." For this, a worker employed a small version of hunting bow and a slack deerskin thong. He steadied the shaft by holding a crosspiece at the top. Then he sawed the bow back and forth, back and forth. The motion twisted the thong and as it grew taut, it forced the awl point at the end of the shaft into the shell piece. Then there was "pump drilling" which is still in use today by Indians in the Southwest. In this method, the worker pumps a wooden cross-piece up and down along the awl shaft.

The metal awls, or drill points which the Dutch and soon the English supplied, made finer beads possible. They represented another advantage, too. They were used to pierce a common clam shell which before had been too tough to drill. This shell of the clam, *Venus mercenaria*, called by the Algonkian, the quahaug, offered a surprising bonus to bead makers.

At one side of each of the clam's two valves is a purple patch. As the shell grows, so does the area of the color until the shells look as if they had been picked up by a giant hand stained purple. For the bead makers to have two colors hardly seems earth-shaking to us. Yet it was a tremendous boon, like the discovery of the printing press. With dark and light beads, Indians could record tribal messages and records.

Shell of the quahaug (Venus mercenaria) whose purple interior patch made dark wampum.

A *wampum maker.*

At first, the coastal Indians wove simple patterns like "checker work" with white and purple beads. Later, the Iroquois up the Hudson wove light and dark into more complex figures and designs. And into these woven figures they wove more and more elaborate meanings. This is important enough for a chapter of its own.

Beadmakers must have taken great satisfaction in the new style beads. When they were smoothed with deerskin and a handful of sand and polished with grease from the rim of a cooking pot, they shone like china. In fact, the French in Canada who bought Algonkian wampum for their fur trade called them "porcelaine."

Roger Williams of Rhode Island spoke of the tribal "Princes proudly wearing their rich caps and aprons—or small breeches —of these beads thus curiously strung in many forms and figures." Thomas Letchford, another early New England visitor, reported seeing: "Beads of wampanoag about their necks and a girdle of the same, wrought with blue and white wampum, after the manner of Chequer work, two fingers broad about their loynes . . . they wore pendants of wampum and such Toyes in their ears. And their women and some of their chieves have faire bracelets and chaines of wampum." In Boston, the Wampanoag chief called King Philip impressed all who saw him enter in full tribal dress with his purple and white wampum.

Until white fur buyers dazzled them with trade goods and wampum, Algonkian trappers followed the wise practise of their forefathers. Their custom had been to kill only a fraction of the animals in a beaver house. They left the rest to breed and multiply. But eager for what was now available the Indian trappers forgot the ancestral wisdom. They took every animal within reach. In a short time there was hardly a beaver left in New England.

So, the Dutch turned to the Iroquois north of their settlements for pelts. They set up a post for buying furs at Ft. Orange at the place later to become Albany. There they built cabins to shelter the Iroquois while they disposed of their furs and gathered trade goods.

They also set up a factory for the making of shell beads. In this way, they always had barrels of wampum to pay for the bales of fur they bought.

As a result, the delighted Iroquois destroyed their own stocks of beaver as completely as the New England tribes had done. But the Iroquois were more fortunate. They had weaker tribes to the west of them that they could rob of furs. They waylaid the great canoes of the Huron fur fleet on their way to French buyers in Canada. When the Huron took up the tomahawk in

Philip of Wampanoag wearing his "royalties" as he appears in a Paul Revere engraving.

self defence, they were all but wiped out. Their survivors fled westward. Thus, the Iroquois of the area could still supply Ft. Orange with beaver from the west of them. As for the French, the Ottawa took the place of the Huron in supplying them.

During most of the years the Dutch held New Netherlands, from early in the 17th century to 1664, they were strong rivals of the English in obtaining furs from the Indians. This is why it is so surprising to learn that it was Dutch traders who taught the English Pilgrims at Plymouth the advantages of using wampum in the fur trade.

CHAPTER THREE

Wampum as Money

❧ ☙

ONE DAY in 1627, after the Pilgrims had lived in Plymouth for seven years, they were surprised to have a stranger and a Dutchman appear among them, wrote William Bradford in *Of Plymouth Plantation.*

He had come from Aptuxet, the Pilgrim trading post on Narragansett Bay. There he had left Isaac de Rasieres, secretary to the Dutch governor at Amsterdam, because the man was too stout to travel on foot through the woods. Would the English oblige by sending a boat to bring De Rasieres to Plymouth?

The Pilgrim shallop sailed for the secretary and his party. When it re-entered the harbor with the Dutch party aboard, they greeted the townspeople with a flourish of trumpets. Both Pilgrims and sea gulls were startled by the brassy notes. De Rasieres visited in the town for several days, then set out with several Plymouth leaders to do some trading at Aptuxet.

At the post, the Dutchmen opened up their chests to show their wares. In one chest lay sugar, that precious substance from Brazil. In others were three kinds of sturdy Dutch cloth. The careful Pilgrims made their choices and paid for them with home-grown tobacco.

The Dutch also persuaded the Plymouth men to invest in 50 pounds (then about $250) worth of wampum strings. The English took them reluctantly. They could see that for trading, strings of beads might be a good deal easier to carry about than, say, bushels of corn. They understood, too, why the Dutch put a money value on these shell beads. Small coins were in very short supply at Plymouth as they were in New Amsterdam.

But William Bradford made a gloomy prediction that the beads might prove a "drugge" on the market and for a time his pessimism seemed justified. Then, gradually, Indians down along the coast and the Kennebec River grew so fond of wampum that they wanted it above all other trade goods. Trade for the Pilgrims flourished as never before.

And so the Pilgrims and the tribes to the north and east of them learned the use of wampum from Dutch rivals in the fur trade.

The Dutch and the English tried to keep the value of beads constant. Purple beads were worth more than white ones because shells with a patch of purple large enough for beads were scarce. Roger Williams, who settled Rhode Island, wrote that 6 white beads were "currant with the English for a penny" and equal to 3 purple ones. He compared white beads to silver, and purple ones to gold.

But the price went up and down, affected by events. At one time, "the Indian wars" were blamed for a bead shortage that sent the value up. At another time, the zealous Dutch produced too many beads in their factories and this sent the price down. In 1657, a Dutch trader could buy 8 white beads and 4 purple ones for his stiver. Five years later, his stiver bought 24 white beads and half as many purple! Some Albany merchants during that period found themselves with a cellar full of barrels of beads worth very little.

How did the Indians themselves regard these ups and downs in wampum as currency? There is no record of their protesting

Wampum-making Narragansett welcome Roger Williams to Rhode Island.

that the same length of beads might be worth less one year than another. What they did grumble about was the variation in the worth of pelts. They were good judges of fur. It made them sullen to have the prime beaver rate fluctuate. They did not understand that the market for furs in Europe controlled prices.

Since wampum could not be stamped with a value like metal coins, how could users know its worth? Over the years many measures were fixed upon.

In the beginning, the beads were doled out by the *handful*. This was a natural measurement, always available wherever there were humans. Of course, a man with large hands may have done better than one with small. A good beaver pelt brought a Seneca 60 handfuls of white wampum, 300 of purple in 1660. And a few years later, the Mohawk accepted 60 "hands" of beads in part payment for land near Schenectady.

Another measurement, the *fathom*, was more convenient to use than loose beads. Originally, it was determined by the length of a man's two arms spread wide, much the way he would hold a yard of cloth to measure it. However, as time went on, the wampum fathom became a measure by count instead of length. Usually, it equalled 180 purple beads and twice as many white.

English traders often used a *bushel* measure. It might hold loose beads or strings of them, or both. John Pynchon of Springfield, Massachusetts, a prosperous fur trader, took large amounts of loose wampum in payment for goods, sometimes a thousand dollars' worth at once. Then he set workers to stringing it for a penny a fathom. One of his men strung 640 fathoms in one year.

A *parcel* is another term that crops up in old account books. This appears to have been a scrambling of loose and strung beads. For the most part, these odds and ends were not "told" or counted and so varied in value.

Wampum was made legal currency in New Amsterdam and in the New England colonies. It is not hard to imagine colonists dealing with the Indians and using wampum. It is more difficult to picture two sober English settlers or two hearty burghers of New Amsterdam carrying on their business with shell money.

Indian measuring wampum by the fathom in payment for furs.

29

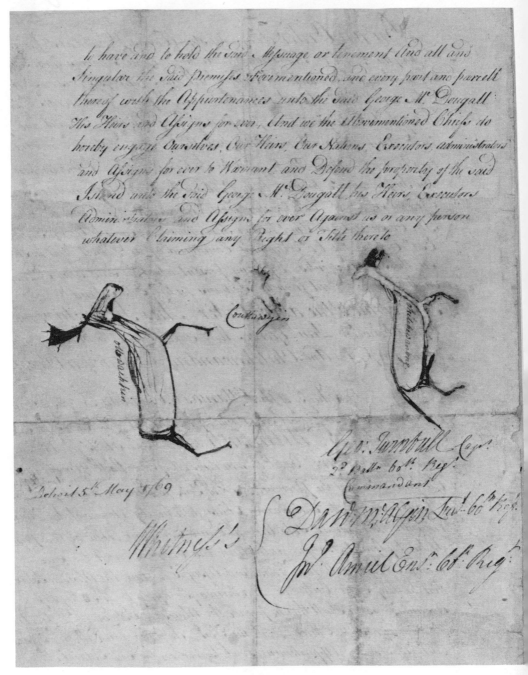

The deed granting Belle Isle near Detroit to George McDougall in 1769. The animal figures are the "signatures" of the Chippewa and Ottawa sellers.

But there were times when neither had coins jingling in his pocket and must pull out a wampum string instead.

Land owners often paid taxes in wampum and sometimes the colonial governments carried out large deals with shell currency. Wampum went to buy miles of land in New England, New York and New Jersey. "Four hundred fathom of white wampum or 200 black," for instance, went to a group of Staten Island chiefs for land now known in part as Elizabeth, New Jersey.

Colonial officials soon took to demanding that Indians pay fines in shell beads. The tribes were fined for breaking laws which they did not know or understand. As time went on, fines increased in size. One commissioner, for instance, added half a million beads at one swoop to an amount levied. Colonial treasuries swelled with beads.

Most tribes struggled to pay the fines. They did not have much choice. As more settlers came from England, colonial governments could send out larger forces to collect them.

What was more, the tribes were becoming increasingly dependent on trade goods from Europe. Soon, hardly a squaw was not accustomed to the luxury of an iron, brass, or copper pot. Many braves had grown up hunting not with a bow but with a gun. When it came to mending a broken kettle or musket, the Indian owners were helpless. They had to rely on white artisans to mend them. This made for a double dependence.

So it is not surprising that Indians struggled to pay the wampum fines and levies. Unlucky bead makers were forced to turn out ever increasing amounts of beads. Sometimes, a coastal tribe might not have shell beads enough on hand for payments. They would borrow shells from a neighboring tribe and set the women to work producing beads. If those neighbors, too, were engaged in making beads for a levy of their own, the would-be borrowers were out of luck. Unless they were the more powerful group. Then they dared to seize shells by force. This naturally caused bad feeling between the tribes. Attacks and counter-attacks followed. Matters were not improved when the troubled tribes realized that the Yankees had a double standard. A white man's murder by an Indian was severely punished but that of an Indian by a white man was easily excused.

In 1633, Captain Peter Stone, a Virginian, sailed up to Boston with a cargo of salt and cattle. He soon sold it and then went on to the Connecticut River to trade for furs with the Pequot. Here, he kidnapped two Pequot to act as his pilot and guide. In their anger, the captives' tribesmen tomahawked Stone. For this they were heavily fined. They were expected to give 40 beaver and 30 otter skins as well as 400 fathom of wampum.

Another time, a roving band killed a white settler near Farmington, Connecticut. Those Indians living nearest to the crime, although not guilty of it, were forced to carry 80 fathom of wampum, each about 6 feet long, to Connecticut officials once a year for seven years.

Several times after such a levy was painfully paid over the required number of years, white officials kept on demanding it. They missed the fat heaps of wampum strings in their treasuries.

Not only governments but private citizens, too, extorted wampum from unlucky Indians. Once, we are told, a group of English fishermen enticed a Pequot aboard their vessel as it lay off the Connecticut shore. They entertained their willing visitor with food and generous swallows of rum. When he turned to paddle back to shore, the mood of his hosts suddenly changed. They pounced on him and pinioned his arms. Then they made signs to the small band of his brothers on shore that if they wished to see the captive again, they must bring a bushel of wampum.

This was a discouragingly large amount for so few to collect but they gamely set about it, making the rounds of local Pequot villages. When at last they had a full bushel they carried the basket in triumph to the boat. The Englishmen accepted the ransom but when they turned over their captive, he was dead. They had murdered him.

It was a white man who originated the barbarous custom of paying for human scalps with wampum. William Kieft, the

Dutch governor of New Amsterdam, began the practice in 1641. His family seems to have considered that Indians were scarcely human. His mother, so it was said, kicked about an Indian's severed head like a football after it had been brought in, following a Dutch attack.

It is scarcely surprising that, in the midst of such tensions, the tribes plotted together to rid themselves of their oppressors.

Sequasson, chief of a band of Connecticut River Indians, planned the death of the colony's governor and his staff at Hartford. He offered a good amount of wampum to the brave ready to rid his people of their common enemy. But the murders never took place. Perhaps no one dared accept Sequasson's offer in those dangerous times. Once wampum was accepted, it sealed a promise an Indian had to keep.

Ninigret, chief of the southern Narragansett, and the Mohican chief, Uncas, both tried a more devious way to rid themselves of white men. They promised wampum to sorcerers or shamans who, by exerting their magic, would destroy the enemy.

Dutch and English colonial governments used extorted wampum to pay soldiers, workmen, ministers and town officers. In this way, shell beads trickled down from colonial treasuries to ordinary folk. They spent it in many humble ways.

An inn-keeper might accept some shell beads for rum or cider in his tap room or for a night's sleep in one of his goose feather beds. A settler might use some to buy himself a cow or, if his garden failed, some "pease," or even a new hat. He might rent a canoe with it, or send his son off to Harvard College with beads to pay part of his tuition. (The college was not obliged to take more than 25 pounds worth of wampum.)

Wampum found its way into the church collection plate on Sunday. What bothered the deacons about this was not that it was a "heathenish" way to pay one' church obligations but that they often got stuck with beads of poor quality, too poor to be used again.

Deacons were not the only ones to complain of "bad" wam-

Ninigret, chief of the Narragansett.

pum. As bead makers were forced to make larger amounts all the time, they skimped on quality and scanted on amounts. Some beads came to fur traders half-finished, some with no holes drilled through them. One Dutchman complained in a sort of litany that bead makers were slipping in wampum "of stone, bone, glass, mussel shells, horn, yea, even of wood and broken beads."

This state of affairs led to laws about what were suitable beads. Stone wampum and white beads dyed purple were no longer acceptable; they must be "suppressed" when received. In Massachusetts, "all passable or payable peage henceforth shalbe intire without breaches, both the black and the white without deforming spots." This was in 1648. In that same year Connecticut authorities insisted that only beads "strung suitable" could become currency. And they refused beads of uneven size that were "uncomely or disorderly as formerly it hath beene."

Early in their use of wampum in place of coins, some English settlers decided to make their own beads. All they needed were sea shells and money was theirs for making. Or so they thought. But the beads they made were so poor that Indians scorned them. The over-optimistic minters gave up the production as a bad job. Even at doubled value, they announced, they would not make the stuff. It was work only for Indians who "are a people that never value their time."

As the years passed, the Dutch controlled more and more production by setting up wampum factories near several trading posts. In those days, the word "factory" meant a quite different thing from what it means to us. Old World factories were not much more than enlarged households of workers. Undoubtedly, even the busy and important Ft. Orange wampum factory was not large. In time, however, Dutch bead factory managers found it almost impossible to enlist Indian women willing to work for them 6 days a week, month after month. Their people needed them to pick berries, gather maple sap, till the fields of corn and tobacco and do a score of other tasks. In the end, not a

A *Campbell factory worker piercing a wampum bead with a bow drill.*

single Indian worked at the drilling and grinding. Who were the makers, then? Not the coastal Indians, the original makers. Thanks to white men's diseases and wars, they had almost disappeared. Finally, it was white workers who continued to produce wampum.

They set up privately owned factories not far from the source of shells. Some, like the one at Babylon, were on Long Island. Others were in New Jersey in towns with fine Indian names like Hackensack and Passaic and Pascack. The Campbell shop at Pascack was the most famous. It outlasted all the others, producing wampum even into the 20th century. Its story will be told later.

Factory-made wampum was known as "Dutch" or "counter-feit" wampum. But Indian users did not regard it as phony. After all, like the first wampum, it was made from shells which were a part of the natural world they revered.

As the beaver vanished from New England, settlers turned to farming. Wampum was no longer needed to buy furs. By this time, too, more coins came in from the Old Country. So wampum ceased to be legal currency. Massachusetts Bay Colony ended its official use in 1661, Rhode Island the next year.

In isolated and back country spots, folk still kept small amounts of it. Perhaps a string or two might lie curled in a cracked teacup for a moment of need. Even in populous New York, in 1693, a person could still pay his ferry fare to Brooklyn with wampum. He could use 8 stivers worth of it, if he didn't have the necessary twopence. And along the Connecticut shore, it was used forty years after its legal use as money ended.

Indians claimed that for them wampum had never been currency. No matter how it was valued or portioned out, whether in lots, hands, bushels, fathoms or strings, for them it was never money. Although they allowed whites to do business with them and pay for furs or lands in wampum, nowhere is there a record of their using it as money themselves.

Joseph Brant, the famous Mohawk chief, said, "Money is of no value to us and to most of us unknown." More than two hundred years later, another Indian, Joseph Nicolar of the Penobscot, agreed. "Wampum," he said, "was never intended to be used as money."

But even without a need for wampum as money, even with the beaver gone from New England and New York, the demand for wampum was still great. Where were the beads going? How were they being used?

CHAPTER FOUR

The Longhouse People

❧ ❧

THE ANSWER was to be found in Iroquois country. Five tribes—
the Mohawk, the Seneca, the Cayuga, the Oneida and the
Onondaga—had formed a confederacy, called the Five Nations.

Outside of this League, these tribes, particularly the Mohawk,
inspired terror. When an English force fired point blank into a
village of sleeping Indians in Massachusetts one night, the half-
wakened victims did not shout, "The English"—they screamed,
"Mohawk!"

John Gyles, carried captive from Pemaquid, Maine when he
was a boy of twelve, found little in the harsh life he led with
his Maliseet captors to laugh about. But he tells in his memoirs
that he was amused by the speed with which the squaws took
down wigwams and packed up possessions when the Maliseet
village heard the false alarm of "Mohawk, Mohawk!"

The Five Nations did not gain power overnight. Ironically,
these tribes who had a reputation for ruthlessness, joined together for the sake of peace. Their wise men saw that unless they
stopped fighting among themselves, all their young warriors
would be killed.

Union was a slow process. The Onondaga, the Mohawk and
the Seneca were the first three to see the advantages. Because

they joined together first they were always known as the "older brothers." The more reluctant Cayuga and Oneida became the "younger brothers" for their later entrance into the confederacy. We have reason to believe that the League was in existence by 1570. Much later, in 1722, another Iroquois tribe, the Tuscarora, joined the Five Nations and from then on, they were called the Six Nations.

The Five Nations thought of themselves as the Longhouse People. Their houses were built with poles and great sheets of bark. Their roofs were rounded like those of a quonset hut. In the large houses, there was a hearth for each family. Fires glowed in a row down the middle of the vast rooms and the smoke from them rose up and out through holes in the roofs. At either end of the building was a door.

The Iroquois lived in smaller houses too, but the true longhouse held many families. Each cluster of houses was protected by walls, some double, some triple, of close set poles. When the Dutch came they called such fortified hamlets "castles", and later the English adopted the term when they took over the colony.

The Iroquois were proud of their dwellings. At the formation of their League, they used the word longhouse as a figure of speech to describe their territory. Because the Seneca lived on the western extreme of Iroquois territory, they were spoken of as "guardians of the western door" of the Longhouse. The easterly Mohawk were called "guardians of the eastern door." And the Onondaga, situated in the center of Iroquois lands became "keepers of the council fire."

Secure in their castles and the strength of their League, the Iroquois led a settled life. In late winter, when warm sun brought sap to running in maple trees and icicles dripped sweet from their twigs, they moved to maple groves to make syrup and sugar. Later, in June, the women went berrying. This was the time for gathering bark, too. The bark could be easily stripped. They carried it home in rolls and weighted it down in ponds until they needed it for building. When leaves turned brilliant in

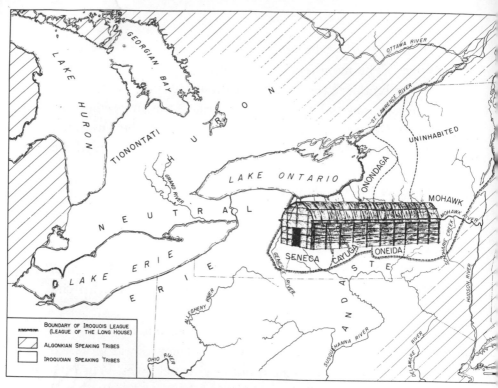

Above: An Iroquois Longhouse and the location of the Iroquois Five Nations in 1600. Below: A typical fortified village of the Iroquois as shown in a 17th century Dutch map.

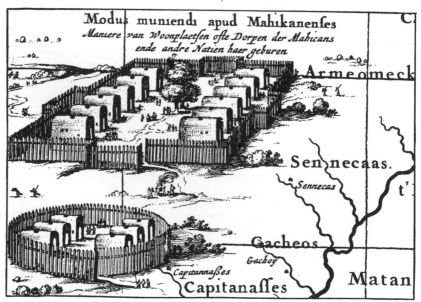

the fall, then men went hunting. They feasted on fresh meat until as one white man observed, "they grew fat as moles."

Two men are given credit in Iroquois stories and myths for founding the League of the Five Nations. Of the pair, Hiawatha is the better known. He was not the hero of Longfellow's poem. He was an Ojibwa who lived farther west between two of the Great Lakes. The Hiawatha of the Iroquois was a man worried by the inter-tribal wars which he saw destroying his brothers. He determined that they must be made to unite in order to save themselves.

Deganawida was the second of those called founders of the Iroquois League. He was a prophet, able to interpret his own dreams and visions for the guidance of his people. In one dream he saw a strong tree, a great white spruce with five roots. It rose up into the sky through the clouds until it reached, so he said, the Master of Life. Among the tree's branches an eagle perched to warn of an enemy's approach.

Deganawida understood this dream. The ever rising tree, he explained, stood for the brotherhood of all Iroquois. Its five strong roots were the Five Nations.

When the League was finally formed, Hiawatha, remembering the vision of the Great Tree of Life, ordered a tall spruce to be cut down. Then he told the sachems of the Five Nations gathered there to toss their tomahawks into the cavity beneath its roots. This would show, he said, that they truly desired peace for their people. Then he ordered that earth be tossed over the weapons and the Tree pulled upright once more over the buried hatchets. From that time on, a symbolic tree stood at the center of the symbolic longhouse. Around its base and before the Council Fire, the League council met.

In Hiawatha's plan, this Great Council was to deliberate on matters affecting the Five Nations of the League. Some nations were allowed more sachems on the Council than others. The total number was always fifty. The men were religious and civil leaders rather than war chiefs.

A union of five nations would have much business to carry out. And in keeping their treaties and alliances straight and their doings recorded, they needed an aid of some sort. In Hiawatha's time, they continued to use age old devices. The wings of a large bird, an eagle perhaps, were sent to another tribe to mark an alliance between the two. A string of eagle quills when sent as messages had various meanings at different times. As a record of events, women wove designs of colored porcupine quills into deerskin.

Then, perhaps a generation after the hatchets of the Five Nations were buried beneath the roots of the Tree of Life, the Iroquois discovered wampum. From their raids to the south and east, their warriors brought back to the Longhouses the shining discs of shell strung on plant fibres. Very soon the ingenious Iroquois discovered that they could replace bird wings and porcupine quills with shell beads. They gave the beads the name *oata* in their own tongue but when they began to trade with white men using them, they used the name *wampum*, as others did.

So important did the shell beads become in the ordinary life and the special ceremonies of the Five Nations that the people began to make myths about where the shell beads came from. And, although Hiawatha was dead before the League used wampum, in their myths they spoke of him as its discoverer.

Iroquois leaders assembled to recite the laws of their League, as they were imagined to look by a French artist in 1724.

CHAPTER FIVE

How the Iroquois Got Wampum

❧ ❧

LONG AGO, says one myth, lived an Iroquois named Hiawatha. His heart was sick because his Indian brothers were fighting one another. Many men, women and children died in these continual battles. Hiawatha resolved that the tribes should make peace. First he would ask the Mohawks to join in an alliance with his people.

Hiawatha set out alone upon his journey. His bow was at his back and his traveler's pouch of deerskin hung from his belt. His thoughts were upon nothing but his desire to end the bloody wars.

As he hurried on, he heard the clamor of ducks. Soon, he came to a pond. As he came near, the ducks flew away. He saw then that the pond had gone dry. Its bottom was filled with shells. He took some in his traveler's pouch. When he stopped to rest upon his journey, he made belts of them. These he would use to make the union between the brothers strong.

When he got to the Mohawks he called to them, "I bring you good news." And he told them of his plan to make peace.

The chief man of the Mohawks said, "We can see the bloody trails. We can see the bad things. Those bloody tomahawks and bows, they must be buried forever."

And so the Mohawk nation was the first to join with Hiawatha in a confederacy. And the wampum belts and strings he had made were used to bind them together. Then the Mohawks went away with Hiawatha to all the hostile Iroquois nations and he showed their councils how to make and use wampum.

A second myth goes like this:

In a village of Indians lived a man and one day in the woods he saw a bird that showered the ground with wampum as it flew. When he heard of it, the chief offered his beautiful daughter in marriage to any of his braves who took the wampum bird, dead or alive.

Many braves tried. Sometimes one would hit the bird with an arrow, but it always flew off in a shower of wampum. Not one warrior could bring it to the ground.

Then came a small boy from an enemy tribe. He wished to try his luck. The unsuccessful warriors did not want him to try.

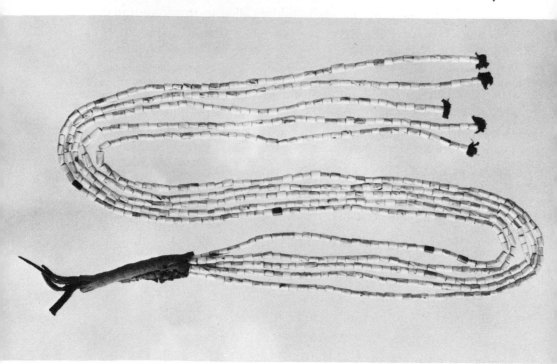

Five strings of white wampum tied together used to open the Council of the Five Nations. Each string represented one nation.

But the chief said, "Why should you fear a small boy?" He allowed the boy to shoot at the wampum bird.

The boy bent his bow. His swift arrow flew and the wonderful bird fell dead. Its plumage enriched the people.

In time, the boy married the chief's daughter and peace came between his nation and hers. And the boy decreed that wampum should bring peace and atone for any blood that might be shed.*

When other tribes took over wampum and the various ways of using it, they began to tell other versions of the Iroquois myths. "The wondrous bird" of the Huron had purple wampum on its wings and white on its body. At its death, it provided wampum enough to fill the largest lodge. The wampum bird of the Penobscot gave a sharp, piercing cry before it shook down a shower of shell beads. According to the Wawenock story teller, a great sorcerer smoked a magical pipe which gave off wampum with its smoke. In other myths, wampum was the sweat of tortured heroes.

It is likely that most wampum users knew that it actually came from sea shells. Even when they had not seen the Great Salt Lake, as they called the ocean, they had heard of it. But as wampum use increased, myths about its origin grew and were embroidered. When the people sat close to their hearths on long winter evenings, their story tellers entertained them. Different versions of the myths appeared.

Myth-making and myth-telling did more than entertain listeners. It tried to explain the world about them and to give assurances that day would follow night and the seasons continue on their orderly route through the circle of the year. It told the people where they came from and where they would go after death. It explained why thunder shook the sky and earth tremors shook the ground beneath their feet. The fact that wampum became a subject for myth-making shows how important it was.

But the myths with all their poetry do not tell us much about the actual use of shell beads, nor their power.

* Both myths adapted from Mrs. E. A. Smith's *Myths of the Iroquois*, 2nd annual report, Smithsonian Institution.

CHAPTER SIX

Wampum As Atonement

❧ ❧

BEFORE HIAWATHA'S PLAN was adopted, the family clan and tribe of a murdered Iroquois man could be caught up in bloody revenge for his death. Like the feuds of the Kentucky mountains, revenge was far ranging and long lasting.

In the interest of peace, it was decreed that after a murder, chief men of both the victim's clan and that of the killer meet and set a value in wampum for the lost life. When a price was agreeable to both groups, the tribe of the guilty man paid up. The wampum went to the slain man's family. This, and the knowledge that they would not be involved in a series of killings for revenge, satisfied his survivors.

Sometimes the amount of wampum demanded was more than a tribe might have on hand at the moment. Then the chief sent out messengers to collect (borrow, we presume) enough from other groups to help make up the full amount. A ceremony of atonement would then take place.

How was human life valued? At one time 6 strings of wampum seemed a fair price for a human life. At another, some Iroquois were prepared to give or to receive 100 yards of shell beads for a man's life, twice that number for a woman's. (The squaws were more valuable because as mothers they could increase the tribes weakened by warfare.) The Huron, the Iroquois tribe living near the lake bearing their name but not a part of the Iroquois League, valued a man's life at "30 presents." Part of them, but not all, must be in wampum. A woman they valued at "40 presents." The Jesuit fathers reported that, when they first arrived from France 700 shell beads were the usual present given the family of a murdered man.

This simple method of settling for a murder worked very well but it horrified the French who came among the tribes in Canada. To them, it seemed that an Indian murderer got off scotfree. They did not understand that to live with the disapproval of his brothers who had paid for his crime in wampum was punishment prolonged.

Sometimes, but not often, the family of a murder victim refused to accept wampum presents. Instead, they asked that the murderer be turned over to them as a slave. They would take pains to keep him alive for, if he died suspiciously, their tribe would be expected to pay in wampum for that death.

When atonement wampum arrived, the donors went through a fixed ceremony as they turned it over to the victim's family. Each separate "present" was accompanied by a set speech. "By this we wash out the blood of the slain," was the first and others followed. "By this we cleanse his corpse," and "By this we put food upon his grave," and so on to the end of the wampum ritual.

From this method of atonement, Hiawatha's dream of peace came true. Feuds and the intertribal warfare that had followed them died out slowly. Iroquois power and population increased, until they were caught up in white men's quarrels.

CHAPTER SEVEN

How Wampum Carried the News

⋘ ⋙

"WASHING OUT the blood of the slain" was not the only Iroquois use of wampum. Their messengers always carried it with them as they hastened back and forth between one tribe and another of the Five Nations, and tribes which they had subdued. It was used in carrying out their business with European settlements as well as running affairs in their own villages. Sometimes, belts woven of wampum or message strings carried the news. They reported deaths and destruction, dramatic victories and treaties. At other times, the messages were invitations to councils and festivals.

The men chosen to carry wampum messages in their leather pouches needed to be fleet of foot and lusty of voice. And they must be intelligent as well. They had to understand the messages they bore and to recite them to the chief man of the villages to which they delivered the wampum.

They must have been discreet and brave, too. Often they went out on secret service. Whenever a chief sent a message which he wanted only its recipients to know, he sent it "underground." This meant his messenger traveled through trackless wilderness to avoid meeting any one. He kept his wampum hidden. Sometimes his way took him through enemy territory where, to save

48

his own skin, he must stay invisible. He knew when "to enter into the earth" on his route and where to "rise" again.

When a belt reported the death of a chief, several runners accompanied it. They announced their coming by calling out, "Kwe, kwe, kwe!" before they reached a "castle." They kept up the triple cry as they ran inside the pole walls. The messengers carried a special wampum string to the village's chief man. When he looked at it and recognized them as official messengers, they delivered their news.

The villagers left their chores—of dressing skins or making canoes or pounding corn into flour—and pressed close to the messengers. Their leader lifted the important string of wampum or belt he carried and from it "read" the news. If the dead man were an Iroquois civil chief, his death notice was contained in a triple string of beads. If he were a less important war chief, a single string told the tale.

Then another string was brought out from the pouch. It told the identity of the man who was to replace the dead man, and it amounted to a character sketch of him. If the new man had shortcomings, purple beads were strung among the white to show his flaws. The Iroquois hoped to have wise men as their leaders but realistically they admitted when one was not perfect.

It is thanks to Sir William Johnson, the man who became Superintendent of Indians in the Northern Province by appointment of the royal government, that we can picture an Iroquois ceremony of condolence.* He recorded one that took place at the death of Red Head, an Onondaga chief in August of 1764. Johnson led a band of Mohawk to the ceremony. Like them, he wore a leather shirt, feathers and silver ornaments. His face was painted with mourning colors.

As they neared Oswego, they joined mourners coming in from other tribes. They all marched slowly on, singing the condolence

* A condolence ceremony opened most councils. Those attending who had lost someone important since the last council, women as well as men, must be comforted.

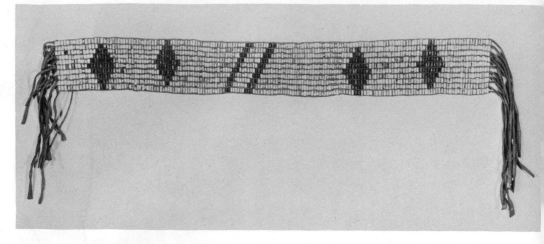

Condolence belt given by Iroquois at the death of a woman colonist in 1775.

song. When the Onondaga leaders heard, they filed out from the palisades and squatted in a semi-circle across the path. There they sat in utter silence while the newly-arrived mourners went on with their song for an hour or so. This was not monotonous but full of variety and a feat of memory.

The song was a prayer to the Great Spirit to bless Red Head with happiness in the land beyond the setting sun to which he had gone. It also listed Red Head's renowned ancestors and the laws and customs of his people.

When the song was done, Onondaga warriors, waiting within the fort, fired their guns into the air as a salute to the guests. Several visitors, stationed with their weapons among the trees outside the walls, replied. The green hills echoed with reports.

The procession then moved inside the village to a bower set up near Red Head's house. The boughs with which it was built were fresh, their leaves still crisp.

The mourners had brought wampum belts or strings of condolence. Now each man laid his down, speaking as he did so one of the customary phrases of the ritual. Each expressed a wish that his offering would serve Red Head's relatives in one way or another. One hoped to "wipe away the tears," another to "clear the throats," a third to "open the hearts," and so on. Later, Red

Head's family would divide the wampum offerings among themselves.

When the last one was laid down, the mood of the gathering changed. Red Head was properly mourned. It was time now to think of the living, and the future chief.

The new leader's badge of office was a pair of "horns." Once upon a time an actual pair of deer antlers had been used. Now, in the age of wampum, a pair of shell bead strings, tied together and decorated at their ends with pointed scraps of leather replaced them. They did look like a pair of antlers.

The new chief would keep his "horns" for the rest of his life. But, if his behavior did not please his people, he could be thrown out of office. This was done in a ceremony called "dehorning."

Once raised to the chieftainship, the new man would carry out his duties as his predecessors had. And to do so, he must know the proper use of wampum. Until he, too, was mourned with wampum, his life would be involved with it.

In dealing with wampum, he needed to be discreet. When some skulking fellow came to him with a meager message string, he must judge both wampum and its bearer. The man might be an outcast from his fellows, acting alone because of a personal grudge. He might belong to a splinter group with a grievance. To give importance to either could mean leading a chief's people into warfare.

So the wise leader would tell his people, eager to hear the man's news, that his wampum was merely "the song of a bird who had flown by."

When wampum strings served as invitations, the date of a council to which the sachems of a village were invited was stated in a small wooden paddle tied to the string. Notches were cut along its edge. Each cut stood for one day between the wampum's arrival and the actual council day. In this way, an invited guest could count off the days and not arrive before his hosts had finished their many preparations and wanted him. Nor would he be too late.

An Indian mourning ceremony as depicted by a French artist in 1564.

But one particular invitation belt carried no dangling paddle. It did not summon guests for a particular time but was a standing invitation. A new England chief sent it to invite Canadian officials to his home. The belt was a sort of woven road map. A Jesuit priest, on hand at its arrival, wrote down the message as he heard its runner read it. "This," he said, "is the road which it is necessary to keep in order to come visit your friends. There are the lakes, here the rivers. Here are the waterfalls."

Invitations to attend festivals, Iroquois festivals in particular, always brought great joy to a village. Wampum strings carried invitations to these ceremonies of thanksgiving and wampum was used during the celebrations as well.

52

The Iroquois gave thanks several times during the year. They celebrated the ripening of strawberries, the planting of corn, and later, its growth in tribal gardens. Corn was the backbone of their diet. They devoted four days to thanks for the bounty of corn, and for bean and squash crops. When all crops were gathered, they held another festival. At all celebrations they feasted to their hearts' content.

Before these religious ceremonies, each person, if he wished, held a sacred wampum in his hands while he confessed his faults and mistakes. The white string for confessing traveled from hand to hand. No one was too young nor too old to take part in the ceremony. He would admit his misdeeds and express a wish to improve. He expected some dire consequence if he did not tell the truth.

In February, the Iroquois had their New Year's festival. Like our own New Year's day, it was a time for fresh starts. New fires were built on hearths. Members of special groups visited houses wearing grotesque, terrifying masks made from corn husks or wood, and special costumes. At the start of this winter festival, a pure white dog was decked with feathers and a wampum necklace. In a ceremony, he was strangled before everyone and his body hung from a pole. It hung there all through the festival. At the festival's end, the dog's body—feathers, wampum and all—was burned. Tobacco was sprinkled over the fire so that pungent smoke could carry the message to the Great Spirit that his people were still faithful to him.

CHAPTER EIGHT

War and Peace

ᦉ᠀ᦉ

WHEN A wampum's message was war, its reception in a village was vastly different from that of a festival invitation. Its coming was announced by the sound of wailing squaws—the voices of women from villages already committed to war. When the belt came into their village its women feared that their men would chose to make war and that they, too, would soon be wailing in its train as it traveled on.

As a rule, a war belt was specially made of purple beads with a white tomahawk woven among them. But sometimes, a war belt had to go out in great haste. If a tribe or other group did not have such a belt on hand, nor time nor beads to weave one, they painted another sort of belt red, the color of war, and hurriedly sent it out. Sometimes a war belt might carry dangling wooden paddles painted a gory red. Each stood for a different tribe taking part in a war.

A war belt could also come, not as an invitation to war, but as a warning against one already declared. One such arrived among the Mohawk on a spring day in 1750. It came from their friends the Mississauga who had been present when a French-inspired war dance was taking place. When these friends heard French threats to spill Iroquois blood with the help of Ottawa braves, they slipped out from the gathering and dispatched a belt to warn the Mohawk. Each one of the fifteen blood red paddles dangling from the belt stood for a warring Ottawa castle.

Sir William Johnson sent out many a true war belt when he wanted to win allies for the English side in a conflict. He often summoned Indian leaders to his Johnstown mansion and entertained them well. At one such gathering his guests "took the war belt, which they painted red and feathered for that purpose and sung their war songs with great spirits." To thank them, Johnson ordered out a barrel of cider.

From this talk of war belts and the Iroquois, one might think that Hiawatha's plan for the Great Peace had failed. This was not so, at least not until the time of the American Revolution. Until then, the Iroquois League brothers did not make war against each other. But they did do battle with tribes outside the League, even if they were Iroquois. We know that towards the Iroquois Huron, they were merciless.

Not much more than thirty years after the Great Peace of Hiawatha began in 1570 or so, the Iroquois were on the warpath. For one hundred years they fought with few interruptions. They fought the French. They subdued Indian nations occupying a good chunk of what is now the United States—including New York, Delaware, New Jersey, Pennsylvania, and parts of Virginia, Ohio, Kentucky, Tennessee, Illinois, Indiana, Michigan, the New England States, and Canada.

The Five Nations dominated one tribe after another. The unlucky Delaware did not dare to sell their own land without Iroquois approval. The strong tribes taught their customs, including the use of wampum to those they controlled. Is it any wonder that in wampum factories fingers had to fly to meet the increasing need?

Over the years of warfare, the Five Nations lost so many men that they replaced them with prisoners taken in raids. The Mohawk, born warriors, lost the most braves. This was partly

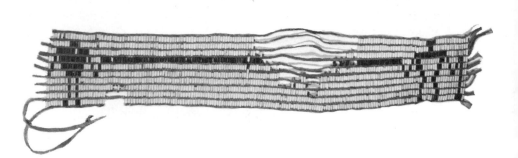

Four wampum belts (top to bottom):
Five Nations war belt, used before the Tuscarora joined the League.
The Lorette Belt commemorating the Peace of Montreal, 1701.
A peace belt with pipe emblem, given to the Chippewa by the Delaware.
An Iroquois treaty belt. The figure on the right is "laying down the hatchet."

56

because the Dutch had recognized their abilities as warriors. They gave them rifles and urged them to fight the French. When the English took over from the Dutch, they continued this policy to keep a buffer zone between themselves and their white enemies to the north. Several generations of Mohawk warriors, their leather pouches stuffed with parched corn and maple sugar, set out eagerly against the French.

But even for the warlike Iroquois, there were periods of peace. So wampum was woven into peace belts. When one arrived at a village none of the drama surrounding war belts accompanied it. There were no wailing squaws or beating drums or dances, which is perhaps why we have fewer accounts of their coming. Some peace belts begged for a war to end, others suggested a bond of peace between two tribes not at war. Generally they were woven of white beads and had a peace pipe woven in purple beads in the center.

We do have the record of the arrival of one peace belt. It went out from the Iroquois in the days when Canada was still French. When the messengers arrived with it at Ft. Niagara, they were blindfolded before they could enter. The fort's defenders did not want them to know the strength of their fortifications. Once inside, the messengers were whirled around as if playing blind-man's buff. When they were too dizzy to tell right from left, they were led into the council chamber and their blindfolds were taken off. Then, dizzy though they were, they had to "read" the peace proposal contained in the belt they bore.

Many belts were as timely as telegrams and not meant to last longer than those yellow sheets of paper. Others were to be preserved with the greatest care. The future of a tribe might depend upon it—perhaps its very survival. If Indians were to retain any lands at all from encroaching whites, they must preserve their records of land sold, and treaties made with white governments. So they committed important records of all kinds to woven wampum—documents of those treaties that the tribes intended to keep "as long as the sun gives light."

CHAPTER NINE

As Long as the Sun Gives Light

❦

ONE DAY in 1722 a Mohawk runner carrying an invitation wampum to a council reached a Chippewa village. He had traveled a long distance to bring a belt before the chief men of the Chippewa. "My friends and brothers," he read from it, "I am come with this belt from our father, Sir William Johnson. He desired me to come to tell you that he is making a great feast at Ft. Niagara, that the kettles are ready, the fires lit."

Whether or not the runner knew it, Johnson, then Superintendent of Indians for the Northern Provinces for 18 years, had a powerful reason for calling a council at Ft. Niagara. Tribes to the northwest of him were flirting with the idea of an alliance with the French. He wanted to forestall them.

Of course the fires were not actually lit when the Mohawk runner delivered his message to the Chippewa. But most certainly plans for the council were under way. Johnson had sent invitations far and wide and 1,400 Indians responded.

Even as the invitations traveled over the miles from his estate at Johnstown, food supplies—barrels of flour, rice, pork and rum—were moving towards the council site in the wilderness. They moved on flatboats, in canoes, and when need be, on human backs. And wampum by the bushel, as necessary as food

58

for the success of Johnson's mission, traveled with him. The Superintendent would make many speeches during the council and for each point he made in them he must "throw" a belt of wampum before the sachems. Johnson knew wampum usage as well as any Indian and he could speak in the same dramatic style that Indian speakers employed.

As soon as Johnson reached Ft. Niagara, he set Iroquois squaws to weaving. And the belts he "threw" during the council helped him to carry the day. He and the Chippewa exchanged treaty, or chain belts as they were usually called. As a result, the English again had the Chippewa as allies against the French.

Eighteen years later, another council met at Lancaster, Pennsylvania, to confirm treaties that already existed between the Iroquois and Delaware tribes and the governors of Pennsylvania, Virginia and Maryland.

The council met for a week in early June. The weather was hot. For a week, Iroquois and Delaware sachems met with the three royal governors on the grass before Lancaster Courthouse. Thanks to a secretary who recorded the meetings we can not only hear the words spoken there but know the gestures and actions of the speakers. We have to imagine how the gathering looked as the hot sun glinted on the Indians' silver gorgets and polished wampums, and on the silver lace adorning the governors' dress clothes.

The Governor of Pennsylvania opened the council. He welcomed them all with a string of wampum. He spoke of the treaties already existing between the whites and Indians gathered there. He hoped that they would be confirmed once more.

"You are our brethren," he said to the sachems and the secretary set goose quill to paper as he recorded the words. "The Great King (of England) is our common father and we will live with you as children ought to do, in peace and love. We will brighten the Chain and strengthen the Union between us; so that we will never be Divided but remain Friends and Brethren as long as the Sun gives Light; in confirmation whereof we give you this Belt of Wampum."

Council meeting before Johnson Hall, Sir William Johnson's mansion.

The Indians gave the shout that showed approval. "You-hay, yo-hay."

Many wise words were spoken and some sad ones, too. The sachem had to beg for help in repairing their kettles and guns. They revealed themselves as completely dependent on those who had provided them.

Although the white officials tried to use the sort of metaphors in their speeches that they knew Indians respected, they could not match Canastego, a Delaware chief in eloquence, wisdom, and spirit. When he spoke of Indians giving away their lands for petty gifts, he was vehement:

"You know well," he said, "when the White People first came here they were poor; but now you have our lands and by them become rich, We are now poor. What little we have had for the Land goes away soon but the Land lasts forever."

His scorn was withering when he spoke of what white men called long-standing claims. "'You told us you have been in possession of the Provinces and my Land above one hundred years; but what is one Hundred Years in Comparison of the Length of Time since *our* Claim began? Since we came out of the ground? For we must tell you that long before One Hundred Years our ancestors came out of this very ground and our children have remained here since. You came out of the ground in a Country that lies beyond the Seas. There you must have a claim, but here you must allow us to be your elder Brethren and the lands to belong to us long before you knew anything of them." Canastego ended in an Indian orator's customary words, "I have spoken."

His eloquence did not sway the governors one whit. They kept their belief in English law and insisted that land once sold belonged to the buyer. In the end, tribal leaders could only accept this opinion. Perhaps they saw that their very survival depended upon doing so. They all agreed to confirm the old treaties, to keep their alliance "chain" from "rusting."

Then, burdened down with gifts, mended kettles and guns, in many cases reeling from last visits to rum casks, the Indians took their homeward trails through the sun-dappled woods.

For almost a hundred years more, ceremonies like those at Lancaster and Ft. Niagara were carried on in councils. Treaty belts and belts of alliance were exchanged and came to form part of the official treasury of the tribes. They were comparable to the white man's state papers.

An invitation for one tribe to join in an alliance was not always received with joy. Often a tribe accepted such a belt from fear. The Iroquois, strong in their union, sent out many alliance belts to the hapless tribes they dominated. But no matter in what spirit an alliance was made, if it were made with wampum, it was scrupulously kept by Indians. The sacred nature of shell beads meant that promises made with it must be kept.

However, there were times when a tribe or group did want to end an alliance. Those planning to do so made it a point of honor to notify the group with whom they had been united. This was done simply by returning the alliance belt in question to its givers. Sometimes, to make their desire for a break more graphic, they cut the belt in two and returned both parts .They spoke of ending an alliance, as "breaking the chain."

When George Washington was a young man and fighting against the French in the wilderness, he witnessed the return of an alliance belt. During the struggle between France and England in America, one sachem decided to switch his people's support from the French to the English side. Washington saw the belt before it was sent back, "the Four houses rudely embroidered" in it. They stood for the four forts which the sachem and his people were now saying they would no longer defend.

No alliance belt had to be accepted by tribal leaders. If they didn't want an alliance and were strong enough to say "No" to it, they did. One chief refused such a belt after its messenger had thrown it before him. He, so a witness said, "tossed it from him as if he threw a snake or toad out of his way."

As far as we know, the Sauk chief, Black Hawk, was the last man to send out belts of alliance. In 1832 the United States Army was harrassing his people to dislodge them from their fertile lands along the Mississippi. Sauk squaws had already planted their corn fields when white settlers swarmed in and uprooted the young plants. Then they planted their own corn and burned the Sauk lodges.

Black Hawk sent out a belt to enlist other tribes in the pathetic struggle to save the land of his tribe. The Army turned it into full-fledged war which they called Black Hawk's War. But his belt was too late. When the Sauk chief died in 1838, he and his people had already been pushed into bleak, unproductive land in Oklahoma.

That belt of Black Hawk's still exists. It is sad to see it and recall that earlier the Iroquois had woven a belt to commemorate the coming of the Palefaces. Then the whites were but a small minority. In Black Hawk's time, they were moving westward in numbers hardly imagined before.

Wampum moved westward, too.

CHAPTER TEN

Belts that Talked and Those Who Read Them

᥯᥇ ᥲ᥯

THE FIRST white men to sit in councils where belts were "read" were dubious about the procedure. Although they saw Indians listening with rapt attention and respect as one of their leaders read long speeches from a small length of woven wampum, they saw it as a means the chiefs used to fool ordinary Indians into agreeing to certain actions. In fact, some white men worked hard to keep a straight face in councils. They would not be taken in by a tribal leader who pointed to a simple sign or symbol among the woven beads and "read" it at great length. They reacted with amusement or disgust, depending upon the sort of men they were, to this hocus-pocus.

But soon the more intelligent and observant of the white men began to notice something. They observed that after a long council speech, one of the Indian listeners might rise and repeat it, detail by detail. If Indians had memories as keen as this, perhaps they also used them in "reading" wampum pieces. From that time the newcomers listened with the same attention as the Indians did to wampum messages.

Today, it is hard to imagine that such memories existed. Our memories are lazy. We are surrounded by devices like printing presses, typewriters, tape recorders, pencils and papers to retain facts for us.

How many of us can report exactly the words of a speech we heard yesterday or even try to hold until the next day the number of a book's page where we stopped reading?

The men who read wampums in councils were called Keepers of the Wampum. They were honored among the tribes who sent out and preserved wampum records. Their role was so important that they always had young apprentices who, in an emergency, could "read" tribal wampum. When the old Keepers died, the younger men took their places.

Usually the apprentice was a member of the older man's family. He had grown up in the traditions of this service. He knew that he must guard the valuable beads that some day would be in his care as he did his own life.

When a Keeper of the Wampum died, the tremendous body of facts in his memory—his tribe's laws, customs and history—could vanish. That was why a young apprentice had to sit in with tribal leaders on the several times a year that the Keeper reviewed his wampums. This reading refreshed his own memory and those of the tribal leaders.

At such a time, the Keeper brought out the pieces from their container. It might be a bag or a basket or a birch bark box. One ancient Onondaga wampum bag was woven of shredded elm bark. It was so soft and so supple that white men, seeing it, marveled that it was not made from flax. It held a bushel, which shows how large a wampum treasury could be.

The Keeper spread his pieces on a sheet of birch bark or a blanket. The boy apprentice kept his eyes on each one as the Keeper picked it up and "read" it. The boy knew that every figure and design woven into the belt, every contrasting bead in a string, served as an aid to memory, and that lengthy speeches or treaties could be suggested by one simple figure.

A diagonal line beneath a Keeper of the Wampum's finger,

An Indian reading a wampum belt at a Council Fire, 1764.

for instance, set him to reciting the right of ways across a certain piece of land. That diagonal line, the boy knew, must always bring the same information from the Keeper, and it must from the boy, too. Someday, for sake of his brothers, he would become the all-important link between such woven figures and what they stood for, as the old Keeper was now. So he watched and listened, absorbed.

The Keeper of the Wampum spoke clearly and rhythmically. The boy must study his dignified manner and be able to copy it. And he must recognize each piece as the Keeper held it up. He must know it as he did his father's face. So during the session he saw nothing around him, not the presence of the listeners nor the flames of the fire, but only the belt as it was read.

As part of his training, he learned what must be done if the wampum hoard in his care was ever threatened. If it was not safe to carry it with him in dangerous times, he must know how it must be hid, and where. And he must keep in his mind, like a map of buried treasure, the spot where it lay. Then, when times were better, he, or possibly his young apprentice now become Keeper, could return and dig it up if it were buried.

When an Onondaga band fled to Canada during the American Revolution, their Keeper carried with him all their share of the tribal wampum. A hundred years later, an American interested in wampum's history decided to test the strength of the old system of "reading" belts. He persuaded the man then Keeper of the Wampum in Canada to "read" those in his care. Then he traveled to the Onondaga whose ancestors had remained in New York with their share of wampum. Both groups had identical belts. Although the two Onondaga groups had not been in touch over the years, the men who then guarded the belts gave the American more or less the same readings.

But the system did have a fatal flaw. In the end everything must depend upon the memory of one man. He might meet sudden death before he could commit a newly arrived belt to memory. Then it became a mere collection of beads. Or, if the Keeper lost all heart for his task, if he saw his tribe losing its lands, its prestige, and many of its young men to drink, he stopped reviewing his belts and even guarding them. One pathetic story of a Delaware Keeper shows just such a decline. He was a chief named Sassoonan and in 1747 he was exchanging the wampum in his care for the liquor of white traders. A Pennsylvania historian tells us," He would have resigned his crown before now but as he had the keeping of the public treasure (that is to say the Counsel Bagg) consisting of belts of wampum from which he Buys Liquor and has been drunk for this 2 or 3 years, almost constantly, and it is thought he won't Die so long as there is one single wampum left in the Bagg."

66

CHAPTER ELEVEN

Glyphs and Signs

❧ ❧

TODAY WE ARE surrounded by glyphs and signs. We read them almost without thought. Some are traffic signs that warn us of curves, entering roads, or that schools are nearby. Some tell us where to find a telephone or a bicycle path. They are as quickly understood as the figures the Indians wove into their belts.

For centuries, the tribes had been giving information with figures similar to those in their belts. They painted them on rocks or tapped them into stone in designs called "peckings." Some of these designs were directed to the gods. If they depicted deer or buffalo, they might be an appeal for a successful hunt. Others might be reports of a hunt or a battle, like notices tacked on a bulletin board or published in a newspaper. The shining area under the stripped bark of a tree offered a surface for communications. Travelers might note for those following after: "We passed this point after travelling from the east for half a moon." Or a band of warriors setting out on a raid might make marks telling how many villages had joined them. Returning victorious, they might report on the same tree the number of enemy killed and of scalps taken.

Probably the Mohican taught the Iroquois to weave wampum. The first belts they wove were too narrow and the beads too large for any but very simple figures. This meant that a Keeper of the Wampum had to memorize a variety of meanings for each one. A horizontal line could stand for a trail or route, like the well-travelled path between Albany and Onondaga in New York. Or it could stand for a journey taken, or a right of way across land. Several times, a woven line stood for the track of a sea voyage made by Indian "kings" when they crossed the Great Salt Lake to visit an English monarch. Or it could suggest a course of action to be taken in tribal affairs, or a continuation of peace.

Diagonal lines, single, double or triple, across a belt were called "props". They usually meant that its senders supported those to whom they sent it. The famous early belt the Iroquois sent to commemorate their first sight of Palefaces had diagonal lines across it.

When it came to representing human beings, belt makers used several bold, simple figures—diamond shapes, squares, triangles or hexagons—for each person or group they wanted to depict. A single shape stood for one group, whether it was merely a small band or wigwam, a powerful nation or a confederation.

Stick figures also stood for tribes, foreign countries or individuals of importance like sachems, provincial governors, or European monarchs. If one manikin stood taller than another, the difference in size showed that, in the eyes of the weaver's people, he was the more important man.

As white settlers pushed their frontiers westward, they built steep-roofed cabins. After a time, belt weavers wove them in belts to stand for various groups of people. Again, as in the case of the stick men, a larger cabin acknowledged a greater power and a dominating nation.

Two mannikins standing with clasped hands most likely stood for two friendly tribes in alliance. A line of them, hands joined like a string of dolls cut from one piece of paper, represented the members of a large alliance. A belt, woven in 1745, depicting

A *chart of Indian picture writing. 1st row (right to left): circle of men; arrows; butterfly. 2nd row: two Indian men and one woman; a white man with hat in his house; sign of the cross. 3rd row: the sun. 4th row: clouds with rain. 5th row: houses; a medicine tent; a pen for ceremonial dances. 6th row: beaver; bear with tracks; eagle with tail.*

A wampum belt, 1680–1700.

a manikin holding one arm out over the heads of six others, tells that the King of England acted as "father" and protector of the Six Nations.

Another way to picture an alliance in a belt was to weave diamonds, squares, triangles and hexagons connected with straight lines. The effect this produced was that of linked chains. Both Indian and white orators in councils used the chain idea and built figures of speech around it. When relations between allied groups were becoming strained, their leaders said that the "chains" joining them were "rusting", "tarnishing," or "rotting out" because of bad feeling. Those concerned must take care to "burnish" or "strengthen" them.

The wampum symbols for war and peace—the tomahawk and the peace pipe—are familiar to us. Once, the tomahawk was used in an unusual way. Iroquois sachems troubled by the great harm done to their people, ordered a belt to be sent out exhorting their men to take up the hatchet against the white man's liquors. Smash all the casks that come into your country, was the message. The belt had a woven tomahawk and a woven cask or rundlet, to show in the most direct way, that war was declared. It was, of course, a war doomed to defeat.

Sometimes, a round disc appeared on the belts. It was called the sun and stood for sunlight. It also stood for enlightenment.

A tribe might send out a disc of the sun when they wanted another to change and open its mind, to see the "light of truth."

But Sir William Johnson dispatched a large belt with a solid sun disc woven in its beads for another reason. His messenger went with it to the Seneca. He told them that they must "carry it to the remotest nations as emblem of the happiness we enjoy by our union." Sir William was not after any change of mind but the continuation of his own policy.

A good many years after Hiawatha's death, the Iroquois wove a belt in his honor. The figure in its center could be read in several ways. Hold the belt with one side uppermost and it looks like a heart. Turn it around another way and it resembles a tree, the straight vertical bar beneath it forming its trunk. As a heart, it can be said to stand for the steadfast loyalty of Hiawatha's people to his Great Peace. As a tree, it becomes the Great Tree of Peace itself. In either case, it can represent the Seneca people, standing as it does between four white squares in a chain. The four squares are the other Iroquois nations between whom the Seneca lived.

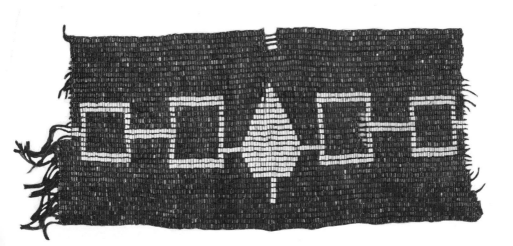

The Hiawatha belt.

This lettered belt bears the name "John Tyzacke." Below: A belt commemorating the visit of a Chippewa chief to George III in 1807.

Gradually white leaders adopted wampum belts in their business with the tribes. The Dutch were the first to receive them officially and by 1654, they used them at Fort Orange. Indians were fascinated by what they called "the pen-and-ink work" of white scribes. Above all, they admired the placing of red sealing wax on official documents. So, perhaps to please them, perhaps to make it easier to identify wampum documents, the whites taught Indian wampum weavers to use their alphabet and Arabic numerals. Some wampum belts took on the look of the samplers on which proper young ladies in the towns practised embroidering their stitches and alphabet.

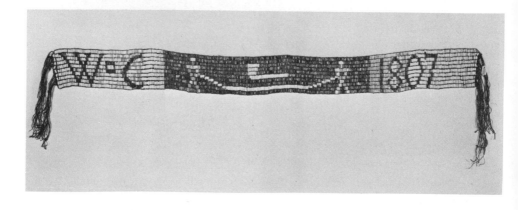

One belt bears the woven date 1745 and has a small orna-
mental shape between the "7" and the "4." Another, woven for
the Delaware, contains the initials GR which stands for King
George of England. GPW stood for his son, the "Great" Prince
of Wales. One Delaware belt has three manikins woven in it;
the largest figure was Tedyuscung, a chief. Two smaller figures
are labelled, one GR, again for the English king and one 5N for
the Five Nations.

Ambitious belt makers wove whole words. In the 17th century, some Christian Huron near Quebec sent a wampum belt
to France. No doubt it went at the behest of Jesuit fathers in
Canada who wanted to impress wealthy patrons in France with
the success of their missions to the heathen. The Huron belt
contained the words AVE MARIA GRATIA PLENA. With it,
went a letter written on birch bark and dictated to a priest by
the Huron.

But among the tribes lettered and numbered belts were never
as popular as those that contained their ancient symbols. One of
them was the cross. When French missionaries brought the
cross with them, they found the tribes among whom they travelled already using it. The Indians continued to employ crosses
as they always had and, at the same time, to designate those who
were Christians. When they wove a small solid cross inside a
larger out-lined one, it might stand for a certain territory owned
or governed by Christians. Sometimes, a single cross stood for
Roman Catholic French Canada. Indians associated French
Canadians with the symbol shining upon their church spires.

Color played a part in telling the message a belt carried. After
a time, beads were dyed to help in their reading. Puritans made
laws against dyed beads when they were used as money. But by
Sir William Johnson's time, they were accepted. Red, green, and
blue dyes helped to convey the increasingly complex meanings
of the belts into which colored beads were woven.

Often, brightly colored ribbons were added to wampum
pieces, too. White traders and Indian traders known as "bush-

lopers" carried them in their packs to the delight of Indian customers. Soon ribbons were replacing the feathers often tied to wampums. Gay as they were, they were more than mere decoration.

Their colors carried special meanings. Blood red ribbons stood for war, a darker red for evening shadows, light blue for the morning sky, dark blue for the sun at noon.

It was important for belt makers to use the two natural colors of beads carefully. White beads were to be used to represent peace, friendship or good will. Purple beads were woven into war belts by powerful tribes. The Delaware, once the Iroquois had the upper hand and taunted them for being "petticoat" people, weren't allowed to use dark beads in any belt. When a peace belt was needed and only dark beads were on hand, it was permissible for the senders to change dark into light by daubing them with a substance like chalk or white clay. After the Indians became acquainted with the light color of parchment documents, they claimed that the light beads of their belts represented paper.

How were these talking belts actually made?

No one living during the years when so many were woven has told us what the process was.

But in the last century Lewis Morgan, a lawyer in Rochester, New York, decided that it was high time someone did describe the process of weaving a belt. He had been gathering as many Indian artifacts as he could before they disappeared. He was troubled that not only the articles themselves but the knowledge of how to make them would soon vanish forever.

One day in 1850, he met an old Seneca woman of the Tonawanda Reservation who remembered how belts were woven. If Mr. Morgan could find her beads enough, she promised to show him how it was done. Finally, finding a few loose beads here, a string there, he had enough to give the old woman. He watched her as the belt took shape.

CHAPTER TWELVE

The Weaving of Wampum

҉

FIRST THE old woman of Tonawanda twisted filaments of slippery elm bark between her fingers. When she had 8 strands of the length she wanted, she picked up a strip of deerskin and punched 8 equidistant holes in it. Then she tied one end of each bark strand through them.

Next she "sprung" a splint of wood into a bow and fastened the other ends of the bark strands to it. Now she had a loom. It looked like a cross between a stringed musical instrument and a hunting bow.

Since her belt was to have 7 rows, she strung 7 shell beads on a thread, one for each row of her belt. Then she laid them across the bark cords. Each bead lay between two. With her needle and thread she took a turn about the uppermost cord and threaded her needle back through the 7 beads. In this way, she held each one in place by two threads, one going over the bark cord, the other under it.

The old woman continued her threading and weaving in this way until the bead tiers filled the length of the cords. Then she untied the cord ends from the bow and knotted them. After that, she covered both ends with a sewn binding. Mr. Morgan

75

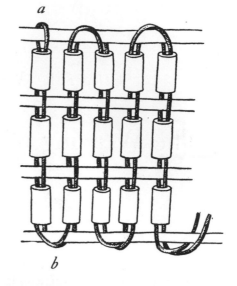

a

b

A *diagram of the weaving of wampum belts. Often beads were strung on a double thread as shown here.*

does not tell us whether she used deer skin or red trade cloth. Both were commonly used.

When the old woman trimmed her belt with ribbons, it was done. Lewis Morgan had his belt and the information as to how it was made. More than one-hundred and twenty-five years later, we still have both.

Although the Tonawanda woman bound the ends of her belt with sewn ends, this was not always done by belt makers. Many had their cord ends hanging free or braided. Even these fringed ends carried meaning. They helped, so their users maintained, to waft a belt's message toward listeners during its "reading."

The method of making a belt demonstrated for Morgan was not the only one used. Another, using a double thread from the start is shown in the drawing above.

Making patterns was the simplest part of weaving wampum. It was merely the alternation of light and dark beads in whatever order was needed to produce a figure. No doubt all the ancient and familiar patterns existed in the weaver's head. For new, unfamiliar ones such as the white man's alphabet and numerals, she needed a guide. We can only guess how these were presented to her. Perhaps they were scratched in the earth with a stick or drawn on a sheet of birch bark with charcoal.

The weavers must have found pleasure in seeing their figures take form. And they found a challenge in matching the colors of beads. There were many shades of white, from chalky gray to creamy yellow, and the purples in their shells ranged from deep violet to white-streaked lavendar. Even the fastidious Dutch admired the way belt-makers strung like shades with like. One of them said that the Indians took as much care in matching shell beads as his people did in matching pearls of great price.

The size of wampum belts varied. The width and length depended on the importance of the belt and the size of the tribal bead supply. The belt King Philip wore when he sat in state was 9 inches wide and long enough to reach the ankles of a tall Englishman, Captain Church, who put it across his shoulders.

This reminds us that not all woven wampum belts were kept in bags and boxes like money in a vault. They were worn by individuals, enjoyed and admired. Sachems owned them and adorned themselves and so did their wives and children. When a sachem wore a wampum belt, he circled his waist with it or laid it across one shoulder and under the opposite arm as a musketeer wore his bandolier. A chief walked with pride when he entered a village wearing a woven crown, a collar of wampum and a figured belt.

The wampum collar, also popular, was bib-shaped and tied at the back of the wearer's neck by thongs or natural fibres. The wide part, a sort of plaque, hung down over his chest. It had the same ancient symbols—diamonds, crosses, hexagons and triangles—that were used in belts.

Sometimes, Indians wealthy enough to own such collars were known to bet them on the outcome of games of chance played around the fire or on wide-ranging games of lacrosse.

One type of woven wampum mystified the white men who came upon it. Was it to be used as a cuff? Finally, they remem-

Denny, daughter of a Passamaquoddy governor, wore silver and wampum ornament when she sat for a British soldier-artist at Eastport, Me., in 1817.

bered that first arrivals from Europe described Indian women wearing their hair tied back or "clubbed." No doubt, they thought, these four-sided wampum pieces with two tapering sides and ties at the corners were used for that purpose. Well-polished and made with purple beads for the most part, they were a fine ornament. It is good to know that some of the Indian women who toiled so many hours to make and weave wampum, had these to wear.

78

CHAPTER THIRTEEN

Three Wampum Strings
and Their Stories

❦ ❧

IN ADMIRING the designs woven in wampum belts and their neat construction, it is easy to forget that less elaborate forms of wampum carried important messages, too. Wampum strings, single and in clusters, were sent from tribe to tribe.

Like the belts, strings that were forsaken by their Keepers or wrested from them, lost their meaning and became simply, beads. The once gay ribbons tied to them, the cut-leather bits fastened to their ends gave hardly a clue as to what their meanings might have been. Whatever ceremonies, whatever stirring events they had been part of, were forgotten.

Fortunately, some strings whose stories are known still survive. In spite of war and upheaval, three groups of Mohawk strings are intact. Before they left their last Keeper, Chief William Loft in Canada, he "read" them for their new custodians.

This is the message of one of the three as he told it:

Many generations ago, the Mohawk clans, Bear, Turtle and Wolf, lived in separate villages. In the village of the Wolf clan lived three beautiful maidens who couldn't meet without quar-

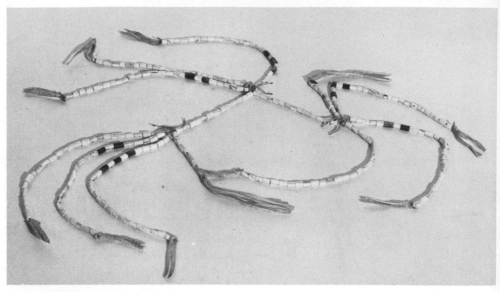

The wampum piece made by Forsaken Fireside for the three maidens.

relling. They quarrelled so continuously that at last Forsaken Fireside, a pious woman, resolved to reform them.

She went to each girl and said, "Come to my wigwam tomorrow. I have something to show you."

The three girls accepted her invitation and each was surprised to find her enemies in the wigwam, too. But before they could fall to quarrelling, Forsaken Fireside said to them, "I am glad you have come. Now I will show you something."

She took them to her garden where squash, corn and beans all grew together in the same hill.

"Look," she said, "the Great Spirit gave us these foods and your forefathers planted them all in the same hill. They are three sisters that grow in harmony. You three girls must live in the same way. Now go home and in three days come back to my wigwam, when I will explain to you a wampum string that I am making."

When the girls returned, Forsaken Fireside held out a cluster of wampum strings. Five purple strings, she said, represented the Iroquois nations. As for the six white longer strings joined to the others and hanging below them, they were for the girls, two apiece.

80

"Now," said Forsaken Fireside," if by your conduct any of you breaks these rules, I will replace a white bead with a dark one in that string standing for you, and you shall be a disgrace in the village."

Then she told them the rules. Each must dwell in love and peace and charity with her two sisters and help them at all times. The maidens stood before the gathered clan with clasped hands and made their vow to keep the rules.

Forsaken Fireside kept the strings with her and brought them out for festivals or councils where the girls repeated their vows.

Before long the idea spread to other clans and similar groups of maidens asked to join in a sisterhood of mutual help and love.*

Did the girls keep their vows? Chief Loft did not say but apparently they did. Not a single purple bead appears among the white as a mark against any of them.

This string cluster gives a glimpse into an Iroquois village. It shows us the concern the founders of the League of Five Nations felt for the quality of the life led by their people. They knew that unless the circumstances of daily life were harmonious, the whole confederation would be in danger of failing. If one small village was weakened by conflicts and unhappiness this link could break the chain of Iroquois union.

* Adapted from *Three Iroquois Wampum Records* by Diamond Jenness, Canadian National Museum Bulletin No. 70, Ottawa Canada 1932.

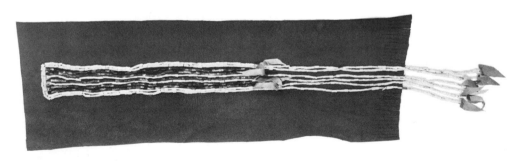

The long single string in this group stands for the Mohawk nation, the short pendant strings for its 9 sachems.

Another wampum record that Chief Loft had in his keeping consists of one long string from which hang three clusters of three shorter strings. The long string has a fringe of three leather strips. The strings as a whole stand for the Mohawk nation. The single string represents the hope that it be united for all time. The three-stranded clusters each represent a clan within the Mohawk nation. In the beginning, Chief Loft said, each of the Five Nations had similar strings. Whether the others survived, he did not know.

The third of the strings which can still "speak" to us is the most important. Like the other two, it has been x-rayed and the 1,800 beads which it contains proved to be ancient ones, made before Dutch awls were available.

This group of strings is a record of the founding of the Iroquois League about 1570. Thanks to Chief Loft, we still know how the League was set up.

Fifty sachems from the Five Nations gathered with joined hands in a circle. The circle showed that the men were all of equal rank—there was no head or foot among them. Each man had a special title and, at councils, his own spot to stand in relation to the others. To help him remember where to take his place, a cluster of strings was set out before a council on a blanket or sheet of bark, like a seating plan.

The cluster looked a bit like the disc of the sun with its rays turned inward. The rim of the disc was made of two intertwined strings. One string stood for the League's Great Peace, the other for its Great Law. The inward turning rays, those 50 shorter strings, represented the 50 sachems of the Great Council. One, longer than the rest, stood for the Onondaga Keeper of the Wampum, a member of the Council. The others took their places in relation to him. Thus, here in these 1,800 ancient strung beads, the whole structure of the League was visible.

These three string records were used at Onondaga in New York until the American Revolution came with its turmoil and divided loyalties. One Seneca chief described the conflict as "a raging whirlwind which tears up the trees, and tosses to and

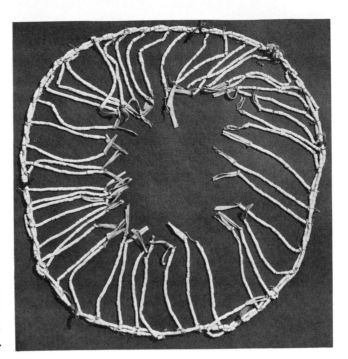

The important string record of the founding and organization of the Iroquois League.

fro the leaves, so that no one knows from whence they come or where they fall." In those troubled times, a man called Two Axes because he wore two hatchets in his belt when he went into battle was the Keeper of these three wampums. When danger was at hand, he buried them in a brass kettle beneath a hazel bush near Osagundaga Creek. Eight years later, when George Washington was president of the new nation, the three pieces were unearthed..

They next showed up in Canada. Joseph Brant, the famous Mohawk chief, had settled there during the war. He had taken the British side in the struggle and could not return to New York state. At Grand River, Ontario, he set up the Great Council of the Iroquois League once again. In its ceremonies he used the strings that had spent so long in the brass kettle beneath the hazel bush. They have remained in Canada and now are in the National Museum.

Of course, they are only a small fraction of the vast number of strings used by the peoples of the Five Nations, later called the Six Nations when the Tuscarora were allowed to join in 1715.

CHAPTER FOURTEEN

Some Famous Men and
Wampum Belts

᪥

WE KNOW that educated, sophisticated men of affairs—royal governors and their staffs and royal superintendents—were not above the use of wampum. Even Benjamin Franklin of Philadelphia, who became a familiar figure at the royal French court, attended councils where wampum belts were thrown throughout the speeches. And he expressed admiration for the wisdom spoken by the sachems addressing them. But history books pass over the part that wampum played in the careers of many of these men and their Indian counterparts. Sir William Johnson should be the first of them to have his story told.

SIR WILLIAM JOHNSON

What could there have been in the air of County Meath, Ireland, where William Johnson grew up, that enabled him to deal so successfully with the Indians of New York? It seems likely that tales of the "salvages" in the American wilderness 3,000 miles away would be more frightening than accurate.

Sir William Johnson, Superintendent of Indians for the Northern Provinces.

Whatever gained him the trust of his Indian neighbors, he made only one mistake in dealing with them. In 1737, when Johnson was 23, his uncle sent him to America to manage his estate in the midst of Mohawk country. Soon after his arrival, he bought some trading goods and went out to sell his stock among Indian villages. He found he had goods more likely to appeal to Irish farm folk than the Mohawk. He never repeated his error. From then on he carried only what his customers coveted—red and white blankets, brightly-hued ribbons, guns and powder, mirrors, kettles and bright calico. Of course, he had a good supply of rum and quantities of wampum. His experience had taught him the power of that commodity.

Before many years, the Irish lad was a wealthy colonist with thousands of acres, the largest land owner in the New World. He built himself a splendid Georgian mansion, Johnson Hall, where he lived in almost feudal style. His home was open to his tenants, his Indian allies, and to any colonial leaders who chanced to pass that way. If an Indian chose to sleep stretched out across Johnson's broad hallway, everyone else, prosperous tenant or royal governor, must step over him.

Johnson took a Mohawk princess, Molly Brant, as his Indian wife. Their eight children grew up amid the activities of Johnson Hall. And Molly kept him close to her people.

His influence with the Mohawks was great. He took to wearing Indian dress when it pleased him. He joined in Mohawk games and wrestling matches, in mourning their dead, and in dancing at their ceremonies. With his face painted, he responded so completely to the rhythm of the drums that to a white man watching he became an Indian.

The Mohawk adopted him into their tribe. And with his dark hair and swarthy skin, his Indian dress, he looked a brother to them. His tribal name meant "he who does much business."

Johnson did not forget his English brethren in serving his adopted ones. He was a Justice of the Peace at Albany, a member of the council, a colonel in the militia. But the office to which he seemed born was Superintendent of the Indians for the Northern Provinces. He held it from 1755 to his death in 1774.

Tales of this Irish Mohawk crossed the sea. London people delighted to hear of Johnson, dressed and painted like his blood brothers, leading them to an Albany council. They were even more pleased at news of his defeat of the French at Lake George. With his friend, the Mohawk chief King Hendrik, and his warriors, Johnson took the French garrison at the fort there. In gratitude, the English made Johnson a baronet. From that time, he was Sir William.

But his claim to fame will rest on his "forest diplomacy."

Wampum use had waned slightly among the Indians in the late 1700's. Johnson revived its use in diplomacy. For the children growing up in Johnson Hall, the arrival of a belt with paddles dangling must have been as commonplace as the express company with a package is for us.

But not all his business with belts took place at the Hall.

Many were thrown at councils like that of 1768 at Ft. Stanwix. At this time, the white man's invasion of their territory brought a clamor from the Indians. Johnson knew as well as they that there could be no peace until boundaries between Indian hunting lands were firmly drawn and maintained. So in that summer he sent out belts of invitation to a council.

The site was at the marshy carrying place between Wood Creek and the Mohawk River. Johnson ordered sheep and cattle driven through the woods to it. He floated barrels of supplies— 60 of flour, 50 of pork, 6 of rice—up the Mohawk in bateaux to the fort. He also sent along the barrels of rum and whiskey expected by his guests. As one Chippewa said on his arrival, their thoughts were taken up "in thinking of ye Darling Water made by Man." And Johnson provided barrels of wampum, both white and blue, for the treaty belts he hoped would be woven.

At the council site, Johnson set his men to work cutting branches to build a bower and rough chairs for dignitaries. The rest would sit on the ground. In a day, the remote and lonely fort became as full of bustle as a boom town. Three thousand two hundred Indians came in from all points of the compass. White officials put on their best clothes and the Indians, when they were almost there, put on the splendid, gaudy combination of their own finery and European-style garments which they admired.

Since there were not squaws enough to weave all the wampum belts needed for the business ahead, Johnson pressed settlers' wives into service. They must have enjoyed themselves as they wove. They were far safer here than in their remote cabins.

At Ft. Stanwix, Johnson accomplished everything for which he had hoped. The participants at the council agreed upon a boundary line and the Iroquois agreed to open up a vast tract of land for white settlement. As the council participants departed by canoe or on foot, there were strong hopes for peace among them all.

But only six years later Iroquois sachem were asking if their English "father" had forgotten them. Was there no faith among his people? White settlers were again bursting through the boundaries set at Ft. Stanwix into Indian territory. By 1774, matters between Iroquois leaders and the Superintendant of Indians had come to a head.

On a hot July of that year, 600 Iroquois, full of doubts and protests, encamped at Johnson Hall. Its master did his best to reassure his visitors. He made a strong speech and threw a wampum belt. Then he suffered a seizure of some sort. He hurried from the council, and soon after, he died.

Although the Iroquois arrived full of fiery protests, they stayed to mourn their brother's going. All there could remember his taking part in their athletic contests and joining their dances. They knew that, although he enriched himself at their expense, he was one of the few white men who tried to understand them. Their belts and stings of condolence almost covered his six-foot frame as he lay in his coffin.

Today none of the scores of belts which Johnson threw at councils survives except one. It is known as the "dish belt" because its octagonal figures stood for the places—Ft. Stanwix, Old Niagara, and others—where his Indian allies could expect to find food.

It is too bad that his "prodigious large" belt hasn't survived, also. When he gave it to the Iroquois in 1748 he was still a young man. He sent it out to the Seneca with orders that it be sent on to "even the remoter nations." It invited them all to join Johnson and his allies against the French. "Upon it was wrot the Sun by Way of the Emblem of Light, and some figures representing the Six Nations," we are told. Beside manikins standing for the Six Nations it had one for King George.

The belt vanished long ago but it played its part in the eventual fall of Quebec to the English in 1759. Sir William would have been the first to admit that this victory and his earlier one at Lake George were won as much by his skillful use of wampum belts in diplomacy as by his military tactics.

William Penn making his famous treaty with wampum-bedecked Delaware in 1682.

WILLIAM PENN

Most of us have some picture in our minds of William Penn, the Quaker founder of Pennsylvania. It may be the smiling face under a wide-brimmed hat that we see on a cereal package. Or a somewhat portly figure standing high on a pedestal, holding in one hand the rolled treaty he made with the Delaware. The sculptor of Penn's statue might as appropriately have given him a wampum belt to hold, for his treaty was recorded with shell beads as well as on parchment.

In 1682, Penn met with Delaware leaders under the elms of Shackamaxon. He had with him a chest of trade goods as presents for the sachems. His secretary wrote the words of the treaty in a flowing hand. "I intend to order all things in such manner that we may live in Love and Peace with one another."

So began an agreement that is remarkable because the white man making it saw that it was kept. The treaty between Penn and the Delaware was never broken while he lived.

While Penn's secretary was busy with his goose quill pen, Delaware squaws were weaving wampum belts to record the treaty. They wove several, some for Penn, others for the Delaware Keepers of the Wampum present that day. Today, we have three belts known as Penn Treaty Belts.

One is know as the Freedom Belt. In 1925, two Iroquois chiefs living at Brantford, Ontario, on the Grand River Reservation, "read" its meaning. Both agreed that it gave the Delaware the right to hunt across land after they deeded it to Penn. On it, straight lines, the usual symbol for rights of way, are replaced by two parallel lines that meander in a stepped pattern. One step is open at the top, the next at the bottom. The lines make a strong, handsome design, like one on a Greek vase.

The two other Penn peace belts convey their meaning by quite different figures. One, of white beads, is woven with purple abstract figures, open crosses with smaller white crosses inside them. The larger crosses, says one interpreter, stand for four tracts of land given to Penn. The smaller indicate that Penn was a Christian.

The other belt shows two figures clasping hands. One is larger than the other and wears a hat. Could this be Penn in a wide-brimmed beaver hat?

Many years after the council at Shackamaxon, a famous American painter who lived in England drew the scene as he thought it would have appeared. Although Benjamin West, the artist, was too young to have seen Penn, he did grow up among the Indians he painted. West's father allowed the Delaware to camp among his cornfields and the boy visited their lodges when he was young. Even then, he was sketching flowers and birds. The Indians, crowding around to watch him work, were the first to appreciate his talent. They gave him color, red and yellow ochre, with which they painted their faces, to brighten his pictures. His mother added blue indigo from her dye pot. With the three primary colors and a brush made with hairs taken from his cat's tail, he began his life as a painter. Years later in England, he painted his Indian friends. Their gay clothing, shining silver and polished shell ornaments were still vivid in his mind.

The Indians, in their turn, kept William Penn in their minds and hearts as unmolested, they hunted the Pennsylvania hills and camped by the province's streams.

GEORGE WASHINGTON

When George Washington was a brash young colonel of twenty-one, he led a small band of Virginia militia across the mountains into Ohio. They aimed to dislodge the French and their Indian allies who had come there.

Washington knew the wilderness well from his work as a surveyor but he had a lot to learn about his Indian allies. He discovered that if they did not approve of the way a war was fought, they would quit in the midst of it. As for his Indian allies, they complained that the colonel drove them "like his slaves."

But he soon learned how to handle his warriors. He also learned the power of wampum. While he was at Logtown, a trading post surrounded by a cluster of Delaware and Shawnee cabins, he threw a wampum belt. By the time he became com-

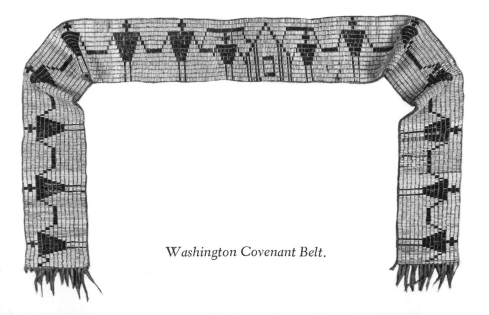

Washington Covenant Belt.

mander of the Continental forces, he was admired by many Indians, and well-versed in wampum diplomacy.

While he was still at Cambridge, Massachusetts, with his army, he received letters from patriots who lived far down the coast of Maine in frontier settlements. They were urgent letters, begging him to do everything possible to woo the Algonkians by whom they were surrounded, to his cause. They were desperately afraid that the English who now controlled Canada would enlist those tribes on their side. Not too many years before, the Algonkians under French direction had raided the coast settlements and those inland for some miles.

Although Washington recognized the danger these people were in, there was little he could do to protect the isolated settlements. He did what he could. He sent out letters to the Maliseets and other northeastern tribes exhorting them to join him against the English. We know that at least one alliance belt went out with the letters because Pierre Tomah, a Maliseet chief, accepted such a "chain" belt and his people became Washington's allies.

So great was Pierre Tomah's admiration for the American general that he traveled with a retinue to see him. They went through bitter winter weather all the way from their home on the upper St. John River in New Brunswick to Washington's winter headquarters in New Jersey.

The Maliseet arrived there on Christmas Eve. The general had other matters very much on his mind but he greeted his Indian allies warmly. He made a speech in the figurative oratorical style which he knew they admired. It gave him great pleasure, he told them, to learn that the "chain of friendship" which he had sent them from Cambridge the winter before was "bright and unbroken."

That evening, while the Maliseet slept after a feast, the commander-in-chief crossed the ice-choked Delaware in a blinding snowstorm and captured a thousand Hessian soldiers, sleeping soundly on their cots.

That particular chain belt has vanished but another bearing

An artist's conception of Washington as a young surveyor. Engraving by G. R. Hall

Washington's name exists. It went to the Onondaga in 1789. Because it was a peace belt, its beads were white. On it are thirteen purple manikins, one for each colony of the new nation. Their hands are clasped in unity, their hats are on their heads, except for one man who has lost both hat and head. In the middle of the belt is a steep-roofed house, looking with its stepped gable curiously Dutch. It is thought to represent the new nation's capitol building. On either side of the house, are two smaller figures. They are, it is said, the Guardians of the East and West Doors of the symbolic Iroquois longhouse. They stand ready to guard the United States' capitol. The belt maker left open the building's front door to convey a welcome to the Iroquois.

The Washington Covenant Belt, as it is called, is now in the New York State Museum at Albany.

KING HENDRIK

King Hendrik's Indian name was Tiyanoga. This Mohawk chief, son of a Mohican father, was chosen by New York officials to go to England on a mission. Once there, his title was stepped up from "King" to "Emperor."

The four important New York men planning the mission wanted two things from Anne, the English queen. They begged her for military aid against the French to the north of them. And they requested missionaries to teach Christianity to the Mohawk. With four Mohawk chiefs as ambassadors, they hoped to catch the Queen's attention. What was more, they knew that the military strength and the glory of the court would impress the Mohawk visitors. They would spread word of both among the tribes.

They sailed from Boston in 1710. Here the plan to impress the Mohawk began. A fleet of naval vessels in the harbor were dressed in their flags, jacks and pennants. They fired their guns in salute and feasted the sachems aboard one of the vessels. Afterwards, the sailors danced a hornpipe and the Indians did one of their tribal dances.

Once in London, the four Mohawk kings lodged at the *Two Crowns and Cushions.* They could not move from their lodgings without throngs of people surrounding them.

They saw the city in all its glitter and misery. They went to bear baitings and cock fights. They were taken to the Workhouse where the poor were locked up and to Bedlam where the insane were restrained. They were rowed down the Thames in a royal barge, all gilt and bright paint, to see the Naval Dockyard and they reviewed a royal regiment in its brilliant uniforms. They were wined and dined by a duke, by the Lord Bishop and by plain William Penn. When they were guests at a performance of Shakespeare's *Macbeth,* the mob in the theatre's pit insisted that they sit upon the stage where all could see them. There were

King Hendrik of the Mohawk with the great belt he gave to Queen Anne.

angry shouts and threats of not allowing the play to go on until they did. The Indians complied, sitting on stage while witches whirled about them and "murder most foul" was committed before their eyes.

On the day of their royal audience, the four kings and their white guides went to St. James Palace by coach. The Indians wore tailored black waistcoats and breeches, woven Mohawk sashes around their waists, scarlet blankets bound in gold braid about their shoulders. All but Hendrik were tatooed; one of them, Brant, was well-covered with designs on his face, neck, and shoulders.

Captain Abram Schuyler was their interpreter. He spoke for Hendrik to the Queen. He told her that the Mohawk "had put away the Kettle," and "taken up the tomahawk" against the French. They had expected help from England. None had come.

95

Then Hendrik, still speaking through Schuyler, asked the Queen to send missionaries to his people.

He presented Queen Anne with a large belt of purple wampum with crosses woven in white along its length. No doubt the Queen, like the four Kings, had been drilled in etiquette and accepted the belt properly. She showered the Indians with presents and commissioned John Verelst, to paint their portraits. Engravings, made from the paintings, sold like hot cakes in the streets.

The Mohawk kings still look out at us from these portraits. Each man wears his court clothes and has the animal of his particular clan at his feet. In Hendrik's case, this was a snarling wolf. Each man holds a weapon brought from home—a bow and arrow, a massive war club, a long-barreled gun—except for Hendrik. He has thrown his tomahawk to the ground. In its place, he holds the important wampum belt given to the Queen. It is so long that he holds it doubled back on itself. So carefully has the artist painted it that one can count the beads woven into it.

When the group took ship for home they had been promised both military aid and missionaries. And the 50 gifts carried aboard must have made the sailors whistle.

Once they reached home, two of the sachem kings John and Nicholas, disappear from history. Brant died soon after his return. But Hendrik kept the center of the stage until his death.

When William Johnson arrived in Mohawk country in 1737, the two became fast friends. In fact, it was Hendrik who took the trail to Albany and insisted that the governor make Johnson Superintendent of the Indians.

Hendrik was very much the warrior as the hatchet scar on his face testified; it extended from his mouth into his left cheek in a hideous, half-grin. He joined Johnson in military expeditions against the French until their attempt to take Ft. Ticonderoga in 1755. During an enemy ambush, Hendrik's horse was shot out from under him. Hendrik struggled up and stumbled through thick underbrush until he blundered into an enemy

encampment. Here the squaws sprang upon him and unskilfully ripped the scalp from his head.

The belt which keeps Hendrik's memory alive is the painted one in the English portrait. On the canvas, its repeated crosses show the loyalty of Queen Anne's allies beyond the "great salt lake."

JOSEPH BRANT

During the American Revolution certain "Indians," with faces painted half white, half black, terrified settlers in the Mohawk and Cherry Valleys of New York. Most frightening about their appearance was that their eyes, ringed in red paint, were often familiar to the startled settlers looking into them. These "Indians" were, in fact, white Tories driven from their fertile farms because of their allegiance to King George. In a savage and drastic way, they took their revenge. They destroyed villages, murdered, burned crops and drove off cattle to insure the starvation of survivors.

Joseph Brant, the Mohawk, often led such attacks. His Indian name was Thayandaneca. It was his grandfather who had gone to England with King Hendrik. Although the mention of Brant's name caused panic among settlers, he always claimed that neither he nor his Mohawk warriors engaged in the most brutal killing and scalping. This was the work, he claimed, of their former friends and neighbors, the Tories.

If the American leaders had been more clever, they could have gained Brant as an ally or, at least, kept him neutral in the war. But Washington sent out officers of such low rank to a council with Brant that the Mohawk's feelings were wounded. Then the "Boston people" as Brant called the Americans, tried to assassinate the Mohawk at the council. After that, not surprisingly, he chose to take the English side.

Brant was a brother of Molly Brant, William Johnson's Indian wife, and spent a great deal of time at Johnson Hall.

Joseph Brant as George Romney painted him in England.

Johnson sent the boy to Moor's Charity School at Lebanon, Connecticut where he acquired enough of the white man's learning to serve as secretary to Johnson's son. Years later, he was able to translate the Bible into the Mohawk language. His education helped him hold his own at meetings with white officials.

Before the Revolution ended, Brant traveled to Canada by birch canoe and took ship for England. What he sought from the long voyage was the promise of lands as valuable as those he had lost by taking the English side in the war. Even after their defeat, the English honored their promise to him. They gave him a large tract of fertile land along the Grand River in Ontario.

Ten years later he made a second voyage to England to ask help for his people. He knew that as they lost more and more of their hunting lands, the Indians must turn to farming to survive. So he sought money to buy cattle and set up his people as farmers. Again, his quest was successful.

To his surprise, Brant found himself the lion of the hour in London. Its people had not lost their interest in "wild men." Samuel Johnson, the dictionary maker, and the Prince of Wales entertained him. And George Romney, the fashionable painter, had him sit for a portrait.

By the war's end Brant was a prosperous farmer. He had between 30 or 40 black slaves, we are told, that he had seized in raids on American settlements. They helped him till the soil and run his sawmill. His lands became a reservation for those members of the Six Iroquois Nations who were displaced by the Revolution.

Brant, while living well, did not forget the spiritual side of Indian life. He saw to it that their ceremonies continued at Grand River and made use of the sacred wampum brought from Onondaga. In 1807 he became chief sachem of the Iroquois.

He became increasingly disturbed by the whites settling on Indian territory. Many would-be farmers did not bother to get government sanction before pushing westward. One after another, boundary treaties were violated. Brant set his heart on having one firm boundary in the south for his people. He decided that it must be the Muskingum River in Ohio. Unfortunately, whites were discovering the Muskingum region to be extremely fertile. There was no keeping them out.

Brant sent out runners with his wampum belts in all directions. He was calling his brothers to councils to urge their uniting against white encroachment. The sachems came but Brant soon discovered that the very leaders who said "yes" to his invitations were those who were also saying "yes" to the white men.

In spite of this, his runners still went out with his wampum invitations to councils. Then, on his way to one in 1807, he fell ill, so very ill that he turned back towards Grand River. He reached home but lived only a short time. Dying, he knew his people to be far from united. He knew they were lost.

Of all the wampum belts that Brant sent out, we can see only one today. It is neither a council nor a treaty belt, although he

Brant's journey belt. The open squares stand for his home and for England, the white lines for the miles between them.

sent out many of both kinds. It is highly personal and commemorates his first English visit.

Three rows of white beads mark the track of his voyage across a sea of purple beads. On either end of it are two white squares. One stands for his home in America, the other for the palace where he visited the King, or perhaps, his lodgings at a London inn called *The Swan with Two Necks*. In this crowded setting near the markets of Covent Garden, noisy with creaking vegetable carts in from the country and the bawling of vendors, Brant may have been homesick for the unhindered sweep of wind across his fields and forests. The journey belt may express more pleasure at being home once again than pride in his London accomplishments. It is now in the Museum of the American Indian, Heye Foundation, in New York City.

PONTIAC

Far to the west of Iroquois country lived an Ottawa chief named Pontiac. For years the Ottawa and their allies, the Potawotami and the Ojibwa, had been supplying Montreal fur buyers with pelts. Two-thirds of the beaver shipped to France came from them. In return, the French gave the three tribes metal tools, trinkets, and warm blankets. So it was not surprising that, when war broke out between the French and English in North America, Pontiac's Ottawa men remained loyal to the French. The chief offered his warriors to their service and their general, Montcalm, gave Pontiac a splendid white uniform.

When both Montcalm and the fortunes of France fell at Quebec in 1759, Pontiac could not believe it. He told his people that the French king "would wake from his sleep" and his traders return to their village near Ft. Detroit. But the French fleur-de-lis flag came down from its staff at the fort and the Union Jack took its place. When two hundred and fifty English soldiers marched in to garrison Ft. Detroit, Pontiac made up his mind that they would not stay long.

English fur traders followed the soldiers. Although at first their trade goods were superior to those of the French, they made no attempt to understand the people with whom they did their business. Soon, their goods became shoddy. Some traders had no scruples about selling guns that blew up in their buyers' faces.

What was more, English fur buyers, unlike the French, refused to provide funds to tide the Indians over the winter until they brought in their pelts. This brought great hardship and hunger to those accustomed to more generous French terms.

Pontiac began to hatch plans against the English. Up to this time, Indian opposition to increasing white invasion of the west had been hit-or-miss. Pontiac changed that. He saw that unless his people made a concerted effort to take every English fort in the west, there was no hope for them.

He gave his personal attention to taking Ft. Detroit on the Detroit River across from his village. On a day in early May he asked the fort's commander for permission to entertain the garrison with the calumet dance. They were welcomed within the palisades. Painted and adorned for the ritual, some Ottawa performed the dance while a few spied out the strength of the fort's defenses.

The next day, Pontiac and his men were allowed inside the fort again. This time each brave who entered had a weapon. He carried a tomahawk, a sharpened knife, or a sawed-off gun hidden under the blanket he wore.

Pontiac intended to take the fort on this second visit. He would make a speech to the English officers while he held a wampum belt in his hands. It was a belt of white beads, smeared on one side with green. When, during his speech, he turned it from the white side to the green, this would be the signal for his men to attack.

But Pontiac and his braves sensed from the moment they entered the walls of the fort that someone had revealed the plan. Unlike yesterday's relaxed reception, today's was tense. Every soldier of the garrison, every trapper in English service stood armed and ready on the parade ground. A drummer tapped a steady, nervous beat.

Pontiac strode on into the room where the English commanding officer sat. He began an angry speech. His braves eyed Pontiac's hands and the belt tensely. The Ottawa chief knew that his plan could not be carried out. He strode from the fort with his frustrated followers at his heels. He then lay siege to Ft. Detroit.

Elsewhere, Pontiac's plans did bear fruit. Ft. Sandusky, Ft. St. Joseph, and Ft. Miama fell to Indian forces. In June, Ft. Ouitenone and Ft. Pitt were, like Ft. Detroit, under seige.

But there were not enough Indian leaders with Pontiac's wisdom to keep the tribes united. His runners went out with belts to places as distant as Arkansas, but the English had armed threats and tempting trade goods on their side. They won over tribes faster than Pontiac could. By 1766, he knew that he must make peace with his enemy. He traveled east to Oswego on Lake Ontario to meet with William Johnson.

The Superintendent of the Indians opened their council with the usual ceremonies. He presented one wampum belt "to wipe the tears from the listeners' eyes," one to open their ears that they might hear," and yet another that they might speak with ease." Then the pipe of peace went around.

Pontiac promised to war no more and to recall all the belts he had sent out seeking allies against the English. He said rather dryly that these would be more than one man could carry. Then Johnson and Pontiac exchanged belts.

Sir William urged Pontiac to "Be strong then and keep fast hold of the chain of friendship."

"Father," Pontiac replied, " this belt is to cover and strengthen our chain of friendship and to show you that, if any nation shall lift the hatchet against our English brethren, we shall be first to feel and resent it."

Then, Pontiac, his cause lost, turned his face westward. Faithful to his word, he preached peace. But his prestige among his people was gone.

Three years later, for some unknown reason, Pontiac went to St. Louis on the Mississippi. He went with a small band of followers and the splendid white uniform, Montcalm's gift, that he wore on special occasions. During his visit he learned that across the river a group of Illinois were celebrating. He asked to be ferried across to join them.

There are several versions of what happened after his arrival. Witnesses agreed that Pontiac drank deeply from the rum barrels. Then he withdrew into the woods and was heard singing songs for the success of his undertakings, whatever they were to be. No one learned. His body with a tomahawk in the skull was found lying where he had sent up his songs.

What followed his death was ironic. If the friends who now rushed to avenge it had rallied to his side against the English with the same fervor, they might indeed have driven the white enemy from their lands. The Ottawa and their allies almost annihilated the Illinois among whom the murder took place.

Today the name of this intelligent and courageous chief is familiar mostly because of the brand of car which bears it. As for the wampum belts, "more than one man could carry" none appear to have survived.

Francis Parkman, the young historian who set out from Boston in 1849 to see the western tribes at first hand, described one of Pontiac's belts so carefully that we can imagine how it looked. It was, so he said, "Of extraordinary size, 6 feet in length and 4 inches wide. It was wrought from end to end with symbols of the various tribes and villages, 47 in number still leagued together in alliance." Pontiac, he said, "consigned it to an embassy of chosen warriors, directing them to display it in every Indian village along the (Mississippi's) banks." The belt said, "unite to drive the Paleface back into the sea from which they came." After the belt was "read" it was rolled up again. Then "the bark canoes of the embassy put out from the shore and whirled down the current like floating leaves in autumn." If the mission had been successful, war drums throbbed in the villages as they left.

The white belt with which Pontiac hoped to signal the taking of Ft. Detroit, like the rest, has disappeared.

TECUMSEH

Tecumseh, the Shawnee chief, modeled his life, so it was said, on Pontiac's.

He was born in 1768 into a life of border warfare. As a boy, he roamed with Shawnee bands that fired on flatboats carrying settlers along the Ohio River. So deadly was their aim that for a time this route to the fertile farmlands of the Northwest Territory had to be abandoned. When Tecumseh was older he led raids into Kentucky—raids that made the Shawnee the most feared of all tribes.

In fact, Tecumseh had a gentle side to his nature. He cried out in protest when he first saw a white man burned at the stake.

He never allowed his braves to practice this cruel form of killing.

On a visit to his sister's village in Ohio, he met a young white woman living nearby. He was charmed with her voice as she read to him from her father's books. He was fascinated as well by what she read—ancient history, Shakespeare, the Bible. Soon the oddly matched couple were in love. Rebecca Galloway agreed to marry the chief but only if he agreed to lead a white man's life.

This made a wrenching choice for the young Shawnee. He was, after all, a leader in his tribe and filled with the same consuming ambition that Pontiac had to unite all his people. This commitment tugged him in one direction, his love for the girl in another. In the end, his people won out.

When, after the Revolution, American forces moved into the wilderness to build a series of forts, Tecumseh led attempts to stop them. He took a stand with his warriors in a wild tangle of hurricane-toppled trees near the Maumee River in Ohio. Tecumseh fought bravely until his gun jammed. Then, with the rest of the Indian forces, he surrendered.

With his people, he moved on into Indiana. Other tribal leaders who could not accept the loss of vast land areas to the Americans joined him.

In a treaty signed at Greenville, Ohio, two-thirds of that state, a large chunk of Indiana, and 16 important locations like Detroit, Chicago, and Toledo, went to the Americans. Worse, Tecumseh discovered that one band of Indians after another were trading their lands to the whites, usually while drunk on their liquor. The Shawnees were losing their best hunting lands. Around every American military post, bands of demoralized utterly dependent Indians clustered.

One of Tecumseh's brothers was among such Indians. He was considered a hopeless ne'er-do-well until one day he had a dream powerful enough to change his life. He became a prophet, preaching a return to the ways of the forefathers. In a short time, it was hard to separate the influence of the two brothers—Tecumseh and the Prophet.

Tecumseh in a British military coat.

About 1808, Tecumseh moved his Shawnee to a new location where he hoped they would be safe. The village was on the Tippecanoe River and was called Prophet's Town. Then he set out to do his greatest work.

With a few followers, he traveled in Ohio, Illinois, Indiana, Michigan and Wisconsin. His pleas for unity won many tribes to his cause. He moved far afield, traveling between Lake Superior and the Gulf of Mexico. And he carried his message to the Seminole in Florida and the Osage in Missouri. Everywhere, he preached that no one band of Indians has the right to sell land which belongs to all the Indian people.

When at last Tecumseh returned to his home village it was to a bitter discovery. During his absence, tribal leaders had given over 3,000,000 acres of land to the whites. Full of anger, the Shawnee chief swept down the Wabash River with a flotilla of 80 birch canoes. He went ashore at Vincennes, the new capital of Indiana, to protest this monstrous "sale."

106

The governor, General William Henry Harrison, sat down in council with Tecumseh and his braves. Harrison claimed that the Americans had always treated Indians well. Tecumseh roared his denial of this at the top of his lungs, "It is false. He lies." But the Americans kept the land.

Finally, Tecumseh went to Canada for help. There he called upon tribal leaders of the Ottawa, the Sauk, the Fox, and the Winnebago. And again, he journeyed southward to recruit tribes for an uprising. He found older chiefs sympathetic but discouraged. It was too late, they said, to turn back the whites. As for the younger chiefs, they had grown up in dependence on the white man and his goods. They saw no survival for their people without them.

Tecumseh sent out bundles of red-painted sticks. They were invitations to join in an uprising against the Americans at an appointed time. But only two tribes, the Seminole and the Creek, would accept. When the Shawnee returned home from this discouraging business, he found supreme reason for bitterness. The whites had leveled Prophet's Town. His people had fled.

Soon the War of 1812 was declared and there was open warfare between British Canada and the United States. Tecumseh gathered a large force of Shawnees, Delaware, Kickapoo and Wyandot, and others. They moved to join the Canadians.

The English with their Indian allies wrested Ft. Detroit and Ft. Dearborn from the Americans. For Tecumseh's part in the success, the English general, Sir Isaac Brock, gave the Shawnee his own red general's sash. Then Brock was replaced by another general so cowardly that Tecumseh called him a "miserable squaw" to his face. The general deserted as his army took a stand near the Thames River. His going left Tecumseh the virtual leader of the Canadian forces there.

He had a strong foreboding that he would die in this battle. Early in the fighting he received a musket ball in one arm. But he fought on, encouraging his braves in a strong voice until a bullet pierced his skull. He died at the age of 44.

If he had been born a hundred years earlier, he might have united his people behind the natural barrier of the Appalachian Mountains. But, for Tecumseh, it was too late, as the old chiefs told him.

No tally of the belts that Tecumseh dispatched by messenger or threw in council was ever made. Only one associated with him survived. It is a Delaware belt of union, dated 1800. It represents the Shawnee chief's alliance of mid-Western states.

On a ground of purple beads five figures, two holding a flag, stand firm in their opposition to the continuing advance of white settlers. To the left of these chiefs, are 7 white men's houses. Off to the chief's right are two simpler structures which are Indian dwellings. Undoubtedly, there were once more—the belt was cut across and they are lost. In spite of its detail, the belt looks hurriedly made. Only one manikin has his head centered and the houses have a disintegrating look, like those awaiting demolition. The belt is frayed and its cut ends suggest the abrupt ending of Tecumseh's life.

The belt is in the Smithsonian Institution at Washington, D.C.

The Great Belt of Union which symbolized to the Delaware Tecumseh's confederation.

CHAPTER FIFTEEN

The Campbell Factory

❦

IN 1735, ABOUT the time that William Johnson came among the Mohawk, a man set up a wampum factory at Pascack, New Jersey. His name was John Campbell. He reaped a profit from Johnson's policy of using wampum in his diplomacy with the Indians.

He was fortunate, too, in the location of his farm where he set up shop. It lay between the lands of the Iroquois to the north and those of the Delaware to the west. It was not far from the shell-rich shores of Long Island and the Hudson River, the main highway for goods and people in that part of the country. He shipped his beads to Ft. Orange and the Albany fur market by cargo vessel.

During the years of the Revolution, a time of great hardships for many, the Campbell shop prospered. It sold more beads than any other to the Continental Army for their dealings with Indian allies. There was as much work for women from neighboring farms who came to grind and drill as they wanted.

From all accounts the Campbell family were a canny, ingenious lot. They were clever at adapting pieces of farm equipment into more efficient bead-making machinery. But they never did away entirely with handwork.

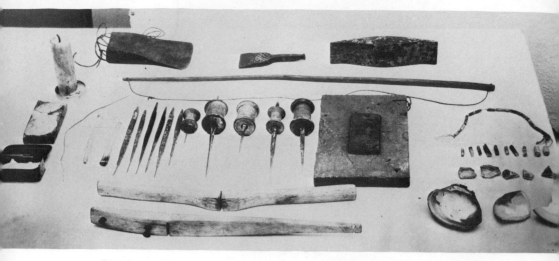

Tools used in the Campbell factory. On the right is an unbroken quahaug shell, a string of wampum, and the stages in between.

At first, the Campbells transported quahaug shells for beads from Rockaway Beach on Long Island. This supply had a drawback. It arrived with the clams inside the shells—many more than the Campbells themselves could eat. They solved this problem sociably. They invited their neighbors for a great clambake. When the feast was over, the factory had its empty shells and the gathering had eaten to its heart's content.

Later, quahaug shells came from Fulton's Fish Market in Manhattan. When word of a good supply of empty shells reached Pascack, the Campbells put hammers and chisels in a farm wagon and set out for New York City.

At the back of some fishmonger's shop or restaurant, they set to work before a mountain of empty shells. For hours, customers heard the quick tap-tap of their hammers. When they were done, they usually had 10 or 12 barrels of purple patches from the quahaug shells. In time, they found a source of white bead material superior to that the tough-shelled quahaug provided.

This source was the Queen Conch shell. As trade between the Caribbean islands and New York increased, tons of these heavy, pink-lined shells came into port as ballast in vessels. Each shell, no doubt, had a hole cut in it for extracting its meat, a favorite food in the West Indies, but this did not spoil them for the

Campbells. They retrieved them from the docks where they were dumped. Then they took the part they needed—the conch's spiralling central column.

The factory itself was a simple building, like so many of the shops dotting farm yards at the time. Except for a tell-tale heap of shell fragments, it might have been a wood-working shop. Inside, it was one large room with small-paned windows. Its walls, darkened by time, were powdered with shell dust. In one corner stood a stove with its pipe at a rakish angle.

When the factory was more than a hundred years old a New Jersey historian described it. Even then, the grinding was still the most irksome part of the work, though easier than in the days of the Dutch. Workers used hammers to tap out shell pieces in the needed size. They ground the pieces on grind-stones, turned with a foot pedal. They pierced round bead pieces with a bow drill. Their drill points were set in wooden spools which no doubt were first emptied of thread by a thrifty Campbell wife. As they drilled, they let cool water trickle down on their beads from an elevated cask. Otherwise, the heat from friction would burst the bead.

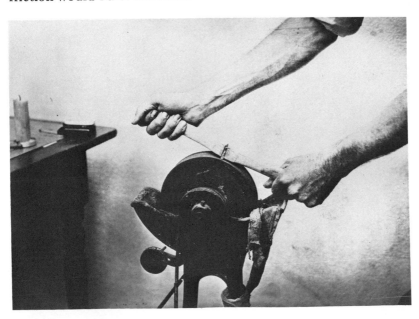

Grinding shell into bead at the Campbell factory.

Several years after the Civil War, James Campbell invented a contraption for drilling six beads at the same time and keeping them cool as well. It was a frame to be lowered into a tank of water. It was turned by a crank. Although he was offered $10,000 for his invention, he turned it down. Business was too good. Traders were clamoring for wampum.

Usually, the Campbells sold beads by the string for which they paid workers 12½ cents a piece. A clever worker could turn out 10 or more strings a day. This hardly made a princely total for a day's work but the family were able to get workers enough.

Sometimes the family sold beads by count, $2.50 for a hundred white, twice as much for purple. The shop turned out pieces other than council wampum. They made wampum pipes which looked like pieces of broken clay pipe stems and shell gorgets and "moons." They also made "hair pipes," so-called because some western tribes wore them in their hair. They also delighted to wear many of these valuable pipes as breast plates.

Once the beads left Pascack, their value jumped. Albany merchants made a good profit on them and so in later years did the trading companies of the west. When, finally, wampum reached Indian hands, it was worth as much as sharp traders with a free flowing supply of raw liquor could make it.

After the Revolution, more and more Pascack beads went to traders in St. Louis, Missouri. Here were firms such as the Rocky Mountain Fur Co., the American Fur Co., and Pierre Chouteau & Co. They supplied most of the outfits heading west with wampum and other provisions.

From St. Louis, the beads traveled far.

When the Army of the West set out in 1847 to take over California, wampum traveled with it. From St. Louis the Army under General Stephen Kearny, moved to Santa Fe and then dropped south to follow the Gila River into San Diego. Along the way, they met friendly Pima Indians and exchanged wampum for their fine fruits and vegetables. The troopers, hungry and thirsty after a forced march, couldn't get enough of the fruit. They cut brass buttons from their coats replacing them with long thorns, and gave the buttons to the Indian farmers who strung them along with their shell beads.

In the process of accumulating his large fortune, John Jacob Astor bought great quantities of wampum for buying furs. Undoubtedly, the greater part of the beads came from the Campbells. Astor resold some of them to the North West Co., a Canadian firm of fur buyers. In 1802 that company bought 100,000 white beads and as many purple ones.

The Campbell shop prospered through the last century. But, when finally, the Indians were all driven onto reservations, they had nothing left that the white man coveted. So the commercial demand for wampum ended.

In 1905, the last Campbell to run the wampum factory went into it alone. He had a new project, to supply several museums with exhibits which would show the stages in wampum making. This done, he turned the key for the last time in his shop door.

What his thoughts and feelings were, we can only imagine. Perhaps he was mainly glad to be winding up a defunct business. Or perhaps his mind was full of the part his family played during the Revolution or in the opening up of the West to settlement.

A photographer came to take pictures of Mr. Campbell at work. How enormously the country had changed in the years that the Campbell shop existed. The last of the free tribes had given up. Their leaders were photographed as captives but they looked unflinchingly at the camera, proud in defeat. Many wore what were undoubtedly Campbell hair pipes and moons of shell. The buckskin garments of their wives were heavily embroidered with shell beads.

When the Campbell shop opened, George II was on the English throne, and New Jersey one of his royal provinces. At its closing, Theodore Roosevelt, the nation's twenty-sixth president, held office.

CHAPTER SIXTEEN

Where Have They Gone?

❧ ❧

Wʜᴀᴛ ʙᴇᴄᴀᴍᴇ of those scores of belts—more than a man could carry—that Pontiac sent out? Where, today, are all the alliance and treaty belts woven in duplicate for each treaty signer or alliance joiner? Only a few survive. Most seem to have vanished like snow beneath a hot sun.

We know what happened to some. Others have simply disappeared. The splendid pieces of King Philip of the Wampanoag, for instance, are gone. Before he ran from the Mt. Hope swamp to his death in 1676, he gave them to his friend, Anawan, to keep. But Anawan, too, was captured and killed. Philip's three "royalties"—his splendid belt, his woven "crown", and the bead necklace from which hung a silver star—fell into the hands of Captain Benjamin Church. The belt was woven of "wampumpeag of various colors curiously wrought into figures of birds, beasts and flowers." When the captain tried it on, it reached from his shoulders to his ankles, and he was a tall man. Fine as it was, Church gave it away and it has been lost for over a hundred years.

We have a few clues to the fate of the hundreds of belts woven in the vast area between the Atlantic and the Great

Plains. Many were taken apart to make new belts. In the early days of exchanging belts, wampum was not in good supply. Even when it was plentiful, a tribe might find itself in a sudden crisis and have no beads on hand to make a belt. Then, the wampum bag had to be raided and an old belt "mined" for its beads. In this way, many a valuable wampum record was reduced to a mound of useable beads, its message gone forever.

We also know that some few official belts were sold off by their Keepers to get money for drink. They may have been traded for food and other commodities, too.

Warfare took its toll of wampum treasuries. During the Revolution, a band of Delaware camped on a river island near Ft. Pitt. The weather was hot. Many plunged into the water for a cooling swim. Although the Delaware were American allies, they were attacked by a force of Americans. Among the swimmers was a Keeper of the Wampum. He never got back to the island and so "the wampum bag containing all the speeches of William Penn and his successors which had been so long successfully preserved by them had fallen into the hands of a murdering band of white people." The story of this loss was told by the historian J. G. E. Heckwelder who knew the Delaware during those troubled times. No doubt more belts were lost in that war, and in others.

Then, who knows how many were destroyed by their Indian owners in their despair and disgust as white officials failed to keep treaties they had once agreed to honor? Many, perhaps, but we know the fate of only one. Cornplanter, a great Seneca chief, led the Iroquois who opposed the Americans in the Revolution. At the war's end in 1784, he worked on the treaty terms made between his people and George Washington at Ft. Stanwix. For a time, he cherished the sword and treaty belt which he received at the fort. But one day, filled with disgust at the sad state of his people and the callous breaking of treaties by Americans, he hurled both the sword and the belt into the fire. Flames licked over the belt's dry threads and thongs and the beads, blackened and burst by the heat, fell down into the hot coals.

Before the American Revolution ended, the Iroquois Long-house was broken, its people scattered. The time had gone when tribes could play off English interests against those of the French to their own advantage. Americans were moving westward. No treaty stood in their way for long. When peace came, the Iroquois still in New York State had lost vast amounts of tribal land. Their chant became, "Woe! Harken! We are finished. The cleared land becomes a thicket. The clear places are deserted." A map of New York State showing their small reservations had the spotted look of a leopard skin.

The Onondaga had fled to one of these "spots" after the Americans burned their village at Onondaga, the historic site of the Longhouse's council fire. They joined the Seneca and hung up their half of the wampum treasury at Buffalo Creek. The other half had gone with Joseph Brant to Grand River, Ontario.

When the last official Onondaga Keeper of the Wampum, Abram LaForte, took over the tribe's treasury, it was smaller than when it went to Buffalo. It was only twelve belts. By 1878, his people saw no need for an official Keeper. The bag holding the wampum passed from hand to hand. One piece and then another was snipped of beads for religious ceremonies.

Needless to say, with their importance gone, the Iroquois no longer needed to use diplomatic strings and belts. Ended were the councils to which these dominating people summoned their allies.

In time, some tribes in Maine found new uses for wampum. In the old days, when a young brave wanted to propose marriage to a young girl, he went to her wigwam. He carried a valuable deer or bear skin which he placed there to show his intentions. Later, he offered wampum instead of the skin or blanket. If he was poor, he would offer only a handful; if rich, he might give a handsome belt or collar.

Soon, an elaborate ritual grew up around betrothal wampum. Among the Penobscot, it involved messengers in tall, silk hats, and set speeches read from wampum strings. A cheerful pink ribbon tied to an answering wampum string meant that a young

Molly Molasses, Penobscot medicine woman, wearing tribal wampums. One may be the belt which was used to ask for her in marriage.

man was accepted by a girl and her family, A gloomy blue one told him that he was rejected. One former alliance belt the Penobscot used to propose marriage still exists. At one time, Joe Susep owned it. Then in 1892 Gabe Paul bought it to propose to his wife. She kept it until Sapiel Paul used it to propose to Jenny Shay. And so it went, travelling from hand to hand, until it was bought for the New York State Museum. There are also several marriage wampums from the northeast in other musuems.

Some few wampum pieces have survived to travel far from the lands of their makers. They have come to rest in foreign countries.

Remember the remarkable Huron belt with the words AVE MARIA GRATIA PLENA? It is in the cathedral at Chartres.

Four other Huron belts were on view in Paris not so many years ago. Another belt came to rest in Rome, another—a purple belt with white diamond-shaped figures—was sent as part of a museum exchange to the Göteborg Museum in Sweden.

At Leyden, home for a time of the Pilgrims and the Walloons, a Delaware belt lies in a Rijks Museum case. It is woven of white beads on deerskin thongs. Eight stepped and joined figures stretch its length. They are woven of purple beads. An alliance belt, most likely. Once it held more figures; but is now cut off at one end. The card describing the piece gives no clue as to how it reached Holland.

Perhaps it came in the chest of a Dutch governor leaving the province that was to become New York. He could not transport the strange sights he had seen to show friends at home—sachems stalking into council meetings with faces startlingly painted, bark canoes low in the water loaded with bales of fur, squaws turning sea shells into beads. But he could carry a belt with him to show and to fix the scenes in his memory as he knew that Indian Keepers of the Wampum fixed messages in theirs.

Even as the belts were disappearing, some of the men who kept them did their best to memorize the messages of those remaining. They read them at intervals and allowed interested white men to hear their recitals.

As early as the middle of the last century, there were white men trying to learn about the disintegrating Iroquois culture and gather the fast vanishing belts.

Lewis H. Morgan, the man who persuaded the old woman to make a belt for him in the way that her grandmothers had, was one. He gathered as many Iroquois artifacts as he could—drums and rattles, bows and festivals masks and wampum belts. And to preserve all he could learn about the people, he wrote *The League of the Iroquois*. In this he was helped by a remarkable Seneca named Ely S. Parker.

Parker was the last man to be the Keeper of the Western

Door of the Longhouse. He was also a successful civil engineer. During the Civil War his friend, Ulysses S. Grant, made him a general and later appointed him Commissioner of Indian Affairs. This last task was too heart-breaking for him to stand. More treaties were being broken by the American government all the time. More tribes were being driven from their lands and settled on bleak, worthless tracts. Parker resigned but he tried to help his people in other ways. He was responsible for saving many wampum belts and persuaded Harriet Maxwell Converse to gather more.

Mrs. Converse grew up in Elmira, New York. As a child, she played with young Seneca outside her father's trading post. She grew to love them and to understand their ways. Later, Ely Parker taught her more about Iroquois culture. After she married she lived in New York City. She looked after the Seneca in the city who went there to look for work. She often travelled to Washington, D.C., on behalf of the Iroquois people. In appreciation, the Seneca adopted her into their tribe and she was made an honorary chief at Grand River in Ontario. Over the years, she bought or was given 10 wampum belts. One ancient belt she found between the stones of a mission house near Montreal. It dated, so she said, from 1671, a few years after some Iroquois from all the Five Nations went north to live near the Catholic missionaries.

Mrs. Converse, Parker and Morgan were not the only three to concern themselves with saving the few wampum belts we have today. By 1898, the Onondaga chiefs themselves felt that their remaining tribal pieces should have a place safer than they could provide at the time. They chose to make the State University of New York the official Keeper of their wampum. When the pieces were transferred to the Museum of the State of New York, forty-four Iroquois went to the formal ceremonies at Albany. They traveled not by the path worn by the moccasins of their forefathers, but by train.

Now there are 26 belts and a few wampum strings in that

Museum. The belts are mounted on linen to preserve their delicate fabric. Five or six at a time go on public view. The rest lie in a vault away from light and unnecessary handling. They are as cherished as two other documents that rest near them—a copy of Washington's Farewell Address, written in his own hand and one of Lincoln's Gettysburg Address.

Several years ago, the New York State Legislature voted to return five of the belts to the Onondaga, provided they housed them in a museum. The Onondaga chief, Irving Powless, Sr., said that his people needed them, that they represented his people's law and religion. It is truly remarkable that over all the years of wampum making by white men, and its use in business dealings, that it still kept its sacred nature for the Indians. Today, old wampum pieces still hold Iroquois laws and religion and play their part in solemn rituals.

The Onondaga belts are not the only ones in museums. Visitors to several American and Canadian collections can see wampum belts and other wampum pieces. On pages 5 and 6 of this book, is a list of places where they are on view.

It is tempting to think that somewhere a cache of historic wampums may still lie hidden, waiting to be discovered. The chances are very slim. It is hardly possible that after being lost for more than a hundred years, King Philip's "royalties" will be found curled in its carrying bag. Yet we can still hope that someday a few at least of the 32 Iroquois belts given to the Delaware may turn up, and that the 24 belts Delaware sachem carried to a council in Philadelphia will come to light. Experts tell us that no doubt all surviving wampums have been gathered in. They say that all known belts are in public or private collections, or treasured by their original owners who use them in councils or religious rituals.

On the Seneca Reservation at Tonawanda, wampums known as Handsome Lake belts are used in ceremonies of the Longhouse religion which Handsome Lake founded. So sacred are they that they are used only once every two years and then only if the sun shines and the skies are cloudless. So sacred are they, too, that no white man has ever seen them. At least, that is the legend.

With small hope of ever coming upon undiscovered wampums, we must content ourselves with studying those on display to the public. If we truly see them, we can forget the cold, reflecting glass of museum cases and the sightseers who flit past with barely a glance. With their boldly woven designs, the belts can still speak to us. As we look carefully, we will think of the men who once read them—men of law who kept treaties and respected alliances. We will admire the smooth polish of the beads, white and purple, and remember that their source was the sea and that they are part of the natural world so revered by Indians. We can even look back as we study older pieces to the days before the white man came, before the need for treaties, to see the women working by the shore, patiently polishing beads for the pleasure they gave their people.

Selected Bibliography

Barbeau, Charles Marius. *Country Made Trade Goods.* The Beaver Outfit 275, No. 2, Winnipeg, Canada. 1944.

Barber, J. W. and Howe, Henry. *Historical Collections of the State of New Jersey.* S. Tuttle, New York. 1844.

Beauchamp, William M. *Wampum and Shell Articles Used by the Indians.* University of the State of New York Bulletin, v. 8, no. 41, Feb. 1901, Albany. 1901.

Bolton, Reginald Pelham. *Indian Life of Long Ago in the City of New York.* Harmony Books, New York. 1972.

Bond, Richmond P. *Queen Anne's American Kings.* Oxford, New York. 1952.

Bradford, William Bradford. *Of Plimouth Plantation.* Wright & Potter Reprint, Boston. 1898.

Brereton, John. *Sailor's Narratives Along the New England Coast*, G. Winship, ed. Houghton Mifflin Co., Boston. 1905.

Buck, John. *What Is Wampum?* Ontario Provincial Museum, 36th Annual Report, Toronto. 1926–1927.

Campbell, Marjorie Wilkins. *The Fur Trade.* Clarke, Irwin & Co., Toronto, Canada. n.d.

Chalmers, Harvey and Monture, Ethel Brant. *Joseph Brant Mohawk.* Michigan Southern University Press, Lansing, Michigan. 1955.

Clark, J. V. H. *Onondaga: reminiscences of earlier and later times.* Stoddard & Babcock, Syracuse. 1849.

Clark, Noah T. *The Thatcher Wampum Belts.* New York State Museum Bulletin 279, 22nd Report of the Director. Albany. 1929.

Colden, Cadwallader. *History of the Five Nations of Canada.* London. 1747.

Drake, Samuel G. *The Indians of North America.* Hurst & Co., New York. 1880.

Drumm, Judith. *Iroquois Culture.* New York State Museum Bulletin, Leaflet no. 5, Albany. n.d.

Eckert, W. Allen. *Wilderness Empire.* Little Brown, Boston. 1969.

Embree, Edwin R. *Indians of the Americas.* Collier Macmillan, New York. 1970.

Fenton, William N. *The Hiawatha Wampum Belt of the Iroquois League for Peace. Selected Papers*, 5th International Congress, Anthropological and Ethnological Sciences, University of Pennsylvania Press, Philadelphia. 1960.

——. *The New York State Wampum Collection. American Philosophical Soc. Precedings*, v. 115, No. 6, Philadelphia. 1971.

Fernow, Berthold, editor. *Records of New Amsterdam from 1653 to 1674.* New York. 1897.

Flexner, James Thomas. *Mohawk Baronet.* Harper's, New York. 1959.

Gillette, Charles E. *Wampum Beads and Belts.* Xerox (New York State Museum), Albany. 1970.

Gilpin, H. D. *Memoirs of the Historical Society of Pennsylvania*, v.vi.

Gookin, Daniel. *Historical Collections of Indians in New England.* Collections of the Massachusetts Historical Society, v.1, Boston.

Greenman, Emerson F. *Three Michigan Wampum Belts.* Michigan Archaeologist, v. 8, no. 2, 1962.

Guide to the National Museum of Ethnology. Leiden, Holland. 1962.

Hazard, Ebenezer, editor. *The Historical Collections.* Dobson, Philadelphia. 1792–1793.

Heckwelder, J. G. E. *History, Manners & Customs of the Indians who once inhabited Pennsylvania.* Arno Press and The New York Times, reprint, 1971.

Holmes, W. H. *Art in Shell of the American Indians.* Smithsonian Institution, Bureau of Ethnology, *2nd Annual Report,* Washington. 1883.

Hubbard, William. *Narrative of the Indian Wars in New England.* Printed and sold by John Boyle, Boston. 1775.

Jenness, Diamond. *Three Iroquois Records.* Canadian National Museum Bulletin, no. 70, Ottawa, Canada. 1932.

Josephy, Alvin M., Jr. *The Indian Heritage of America.* Bantam, New York. 1969.

————. *The Patriot Chiefs.* Viking Compass, New York. 1969.

Josselyn, John. *Account of Two Voyages to New England.* W. Veazie, Boston. Reprint, 1865.

Kellogg, Capt. Martin. Letter from, in *The Wolcott Papers,* v. xvi. Collections of the Connecticut Historical Society, n.d.

Keppler, Joseph. *The Peace Tomahawk Algonkian Wampum Indian Notes,* v. 6, New York. 1929.

Kidder, Frederic. *Military Operations of Eastern Maine and Nova Scotia in the Revolution.* Joel Munsell, Albany. 1867.

LaFarge, Oliver. *The Pictorial History of the American Indian.* Crown, New York, 1956.

Leach, Douglas E. *Flintlock and Tomahawk.* Norton, New York. 1966.

Morgan, Lewis H. *League of the Iroquois.* Citadel, Secaucus, New Jersey. Reprint, 1972.

Morris, Percy A. *A Field Guide to the Shells.* Houghton Mifflin Co., Boston. 1951.

Morton, Thomas. *The New English Canaan.* Prince Society, Boston. Reprint, 1883.

Myrtle, Minnie. *The Iroquois.* Appleton, New York. 1855.

Nicolar, Joseph. *The Life and Tradition of the Red Man.* Bangor, Maine. 1893.

O'Callaghan, Edmund B., editor. *Documents Relative to the Colonial History of the State of New York,* v. 4, 7, 13. Albany. 1868.

Orchard, William C. *The Penn Wampum Belts.* Museum of the American Indian, Heye Foundation, Leaflet 4, New York. 1925.

Parkman, Francis. *France and England in North America,* edited by S. E. Morison. Faber and Faber, London. 1956.

————. *The Conspiracy of Pontiac.* Boston. 1870.

Raymond, W. O. *The River St. John.* Tribune Press, Sackville, N.B., Canada. 1950.

Ritchie, William A. *Indian History of New York State,* I The Iroquoian Tribes, Part II *The Algonkian Tribes.* State Museum and Science Service, Albany. n.d.

Schoolcraft, H. R. *Notes on the Iroquois.* New York. 1846.

Smith, Mrs. E. A. *Myths of the Iroquois.* Smithsonian Institution, Bureau of Ethnology, 2nd Annual Report, Washington.

Speck, Frank G. *The Pennsylvania Wampum Belts.* Museum of the American Indian, Heye Foundation, Leaflet 4, New York. Mar. 22, 1925.

————. *The Iroquois.* Cranbrook Institute of Science, Bulletin 23, Bloomfield Hills, Michigan. 1955.

Taxay, Don. *Money of the American Indians.* Nummus, Flushing, N.Y. 1970.

Van der Donck, Adrien. *Description of New Netherlands.* New York Historical Collections, series 2, v. 1, New York. 1841.

Wallace, Anthony F. C. *The Death and Rebirth of the Seneca.* Knopf, New York. 1970.

Welles, Edwin Stanley, *Some Notes on Wampum.* Privately printed, Newington Connecticut. 1924.

Weslager, C. A. *The Delaware Indians.* Rutgers University, Rutgers, New Jersey. 1972.

Whiteford, Andrew Hunter. *North American Indian Arts.* Golden Press, New York. 1970.

Wilson, Edmund. *Apologies to the Iroquois.* Farrar, Strauss & Giroux, New York. 1970.

Winthrop, John. *A History of New England from 1630 to 1649,* ed. by John Savage. Boston. 1825.

Wood, William. *New England's Prospect.* E. M. Boynton, Boston. Reprint, 1898.

Index